F·A·

to do with me.

Matthew Law.

Printed in the United Kingdom

Published by Duality Books.

www.dualitybooks.com

website: www.matthewlaw.co.uk
email: matthewlaw@hotmail.co.uk
facebook: Matthew Law
twitter: matthewlaw1968

With thanks to -

Francoise Stevens Photography, for the cover photo.

Ataxia UK

Donna Smith

Graham Johnson

John Ebbs

Katie Henderson

Louise Perry

Miriam Broadway

Pam Law

Patricia Venus

Terry Law

Victoria Slatter

Chapters.

Foreword. Page 5.

Chapter 1. - My Background. Page 10.

Chapter 2 - Then and Now. Page 17.

Chapter 3 - My Driving. Page 24.

Chapter 4 - My Travels. Page 41.

Chapter 5 - My PAs. Page 49.

Chapter 6 - My Special Home. Page 56.

Chapter 7 - Two Diagnoses. Page 65.

Chapter 8 - My Family. Page 75.

Chapter 9 - My Friends And My School Life. Page 125.

Chapter 10 - My Diaries. Page 136.

Chapter 11 - My Relationships. Page 143.

Chapter 12 - My Working Life. Page 154.

Chapter 13 - Decision Time. Page 167.

Chapter 14 - Ataxia UK. Page 175.

Chapter 15 - My Spanish Home. Page 180.

Chapter 16. My Future. Page 185.

Foreword

What is ataxia?

The etymology of the word ataxia - From the Greek *a-*, a privative prefix, + *taxis* "arrangement, order" from the stem of *tassein* - "to arrange".

I don't want to bore people with a ton of medical stuff but I think for those who a) have no knowledge at all and b) may be struggling with a range of symptoms, a brief description may help. Ataxia is in fact not just one condition but many; mine of course is Friedreich's Ataxia (FA), so I will focus on this as it forms the background to my story, the one you are about to read. The posh description for this condition is that of an *autosomal recessive inherited disease,* which in lay-person's terms means a genetic condition present in the autosomes i.e. the non sex determining chromosomes, and what makes it recessive is the fact that both parents pass the genetic trait on to a child through being carriers rather than having the condition themselves.

The disease manifests itself in many ways and at varying ages. Some of the more typical ones are: Nerve damage with a resulting loss of coordination and balance; visual and hearing impairment; slurred speech; curvature of the spine and deformity in the feet. Other more serious conditions can be diabetes and a variety of heart conditions.

In order to make the rest of your body move, your brain sends messages to it via nerve cells. Basically a message leaves the brain and then it is passed from one nerve cell to the next and so on until it reaches wherever it needs to go, but in my body the nerve cells that carry these messages have progressively become damaged. I move in a very awkward and uncoordinated way because the messages are mixed-up. It's like your brain and the rest of your body being on two ends of a telephone conversation. Both parties are talking and listening as they should be, with the brain telling the body what to do and the body telling the brain that it has done it. But the telephone wire (which reads like the nerve cells carrying the messages) has become nicked and knotted and the conversation becomes jumbled up.

Why does this happen? Well FA is recessively inherited. You have two copies of every gene in your body: one from your mum and one from your dad. There are about 24,000 genes in our bodies, and they define who we are. With something that's recessive, be it FA or colour blindness, you need both copies of the gene to stand a chance of inheriting that particular trait. If only one copy of the gene is present but the other isn't, then you will not inherit that trait. In my body both copies of the FA gene are faulty - there is no 'good' copy to override the faulty FA one.

The faulty FA gene has a mistake in its DNA and my body is instructed to make too little of a protein called Frataxin. Frataxin is involved in the process by which cells make energy. A reduction in frataxin protein leads to less energy made, more damaging 'free radicals' and a damaging accumulation of iron within a particular part of the cell. All this leads to damage to the cells. The cells mostly affected are nerve cells, but cells in the pancreas and heart can be affected too causing diabetes and cardiomyopathy.

Ataxia UK, like its sister organisations around the world, funds a range of research projects including basic science research, applied research such as pilot trials testing treatments. The charity believes in a hands-on approach to research with its body of members being asked to assist in projects. The ultimate aim is finding treatments and cures for the ataxias, whilst at the same time supporting people living with ataxia. The charity has also set up specialist ataxia centres around the UK, which are clinics providing specialist diagnosis and treatment for the ataxias. Ataxia UK is also active internationally being part of the umbrella organisation of European Ataxia charities, euro-ATAXIA and working collaboratively with charities in Europe and in the US.

Although research and medical care is of utmost importance we must not forget about the psychological and emotional impact of the disease, something which is important both for people with ataxia and their families. A paper was published in 2010 that details the effect of FA on people (V. Brook White et al., (2010) **'Exploration of transitional life events in individuals with Friedreich's Ataxia: Implications for genetic counselling.'** The researchers say,

'Friedreich's Ataxia increased the complexity and magnitude of transitional events for study participants. Transitional events commonly represented significant loss and presented challenges to self-esteem and identity. Findings from this study help alert professionals of potentially challenging times in patients' lives, which are influenced by chronic illness or disability....'

FA is pretty rare - 1 in 40,000 in the UK (that means there are about 1,500 people who have FA in this country). However, to put some kind of perspective on it, it is interesting to think that as few as 1 in 100 of us are carriers of this rogue gene. The chances of having children with another carrier is thus 1 in 10,000 and you have a 1 in 4 chance of your child being affected. There are about 40,000 people who follow Chelsea at each home match and on average one of them has Friedreich's Ataxia (me!). However, on average, 400 of these people will be carriers. I don't really like having something that nobody knows about, so one of the reasons for writing this book is that it makes me feel that I'm raising awareness in a small way.

There is no known cure although research continues and who knows the developments being made may help people in the future. However, there are some ways to treat a person with FA and other ataxias such as medications for muscle spasms, surgery for scoliosis, and a standing frame to alleviate complications from constant wheelchair use, medications for heart and other disorders and a range of exercise programmes developed by physiotherapists. Speech and language therapists and occupational therapists can also provide help for speech and swallowing complications and adaptations to the home etc.

7

My daily exercise routine is as follows:

- A five minute medi-motion leg cycle warm up
- A twenty minute level 2 leg cycle
- A five minute leg warm down
- A ten minute arm workout on my medi-motion cycle
- A thirty minute standing session in my frame.

Once a week routine is as follows:

I see a Physiotherapist (well, a PA who does physiotherapy) once a week where I lie face down on a bed and lift my legs bending my knees, I also have my legs bent up from the knee and push down against the resistance. Later I do leg stretches when in my chair and leg lifts from the height of an exercise step, lifting my legs four times as high as I can. This takes around 30 minutes.

I attend a yearly outpatient's appointment at one of the specialist ataxia centres I mentioned just now and am partaking in EFACTS (the European Friedreich's Ataxia Consortium for Translational Studies). People who have Friedreich's Ataxia and clinical specialists are dispersed all around Europe. This is a hindrance for patients to receive the care they need, and for clinicians and researchers to make progress. EFACTS has been created to move past this limitation. I also take daily vitamin supplements namely Co-Q10 and Vitamin E, as recommended by the ataxia centre, and a multivitamin and Vitamin C during the winter months to help me steer clear of colds.

I feel I am doing my bit - sort of helping myself. When people tell me they are having difficulty moving I advise exercise - I know it has kept me going. When I first retired from work, I said it was important to keep body and mind working. This activates the former.

My experience of FA has seen some of the symptoms mentioned above manifest themselves and as a result I do engage in a regular and rigorous exercise regime and that coupled with my determination has meant that I am still active in life and as mobile as I can be. This book details some of my fights to keep going and my journey to what I describe as an independent life.

Chapter 1.
My Background.

I had a totally and absolutely normal, one could even say, standard family life as a child [Pics 30 31 & 33]. Ours was just a normal family, living in the usual 3 bedroom semidetached house. Dad worked full-time as a Shipping Representative, basically selling space on ships to companies wishing to export their goods and mum worked part time in the local post office whilst bringing us up. Mum's part-time job was actually a full time post which she shared with a friend of hers called Pauline. When mum was at the post office, we would stay at Pauline's and when Pauline was at the post office we would be at home. Pauline's children, Alison and Ian, were similar ages to us so it worked well. Pauline lived just a few doors up from us on Gloucester Road in Bagshot. Mum and dad still live in the same house to this day. We moved there from Fulham when I was just two months old. Neither Pauline, Alison, Ian nor any of my family or friends could have had the slightest idea how my life, when aged 13, would gradually change into what it is today.

My only real physical problems until then were with my eyes. I was becoming very short sighted and needed glasses from the age of 13, and with my ears that regularly filled with earwax which had to be syringed out every six months. With my eyes and as is probably very common as a child, I hated wearing glasses for a good few years and would only wear them when I absolutely had to. I chose to move closer to the front of the classroom to be able to see the blackboard without the need to put them on, rather than remain with my friends at the back with my glasses on. I soon grew out of that though and was wearing them all the time from the age of 15. I was by this time playing a lot of snooker which caused me huge problems in that I could see either the cue ball or the object ball but not both as I addressed the ball keeping my head as still as possible. I struggled on with this 'which ball do I need to see more clearly' conundrum for three or four years until I started to think about wearing contact lenses. I got on brilliantly with them and loved the freedom they gave me, especially playing snooker. Over the years, and due to the increased finger dexterity problems that ataxia brings, it was becoming more and more difficult to keep putting in and taking out my lenses. I continued though for many years and even changed from the ones you had to remove every night to the 'higher water based content' ones that you could sleep in every day for a month before replacing them. In 2007 when 38 I had laser eye treatment which solved my short sightedness for good. Only for me to become long sighted at 44 and require reading glasses! Still, it was nice to need no artificial vision adjustment for 6 years!

Going back to my family....we were a close knit unit. I respected my dad not least because he was a good sportsman like his father before him and that impressed me a lot. My mum too was a keen sportswoman and from a sporting family and I respected her. My sister and I had our fights like many siblings do, which may have had to do with how we were perceived back then by others, apparently I was always a 'good boy' and she was a 'naughty girl'. No wonder then that jealousies and annoyances developed between us.

I used to go to Butlins in Bognor Regis regularly throughout my childhood with my maternal grandparents and my only maternal cousin Austen. Each summer during the school holidays we would set off from our homes. Grandad would drive, very badly, down the long, narrow, bendy roads to the south coast. Every year there were arguments in the car between nan and grandad as to the best route and I'm sure that although the route was similar, it was slightly different each year. Once we had arrived everything was fine and I would play table tennis with them both which I enjoyed a lot. They both played well into their 70's. I also played snooker in the evenings at the holiday camp with grandad. Grandad liked the sport so much that he got a small table in their home. As they lived close by I would often pop round with a mate to have a game.

Walter, or Wally as he was known, my dad's father, had been a keen boxer in his younger days and loved to watch cricket and football. Dad talks about the time when his father first took him to a Chelsea match when he was still a young boy. So you can see why the club mean so much to me.

Without doubt my biggest interest is Chelsea Football Club. I have been a season ticket holder since the 1987/88 season and have now been regularly attending matches at Stamford Bridge for over 30 years. So 'why Chelsea?' I hear you ask. Well, to say 'because I was born there' seems a rather vague reason. The statement is true however but it is not really a reason in itself is it? I guess the best answer to the question is quite simply that my dad started taking me regularly to watch Chelsea when I was a boy of 11 or 12. My dad is a Chelsea fan because his dad took him as a boy as I mentioned before. So when I say Chelsea is in my blood it is probably as near as you can get. My first Chelsea hero was Steve Finnieston and his last game for the club was in April 1978. I am not sure what my first match was but I can remember seeing players like Graham and Ray Wilkins, Micky Droy, Ian Britton and Ray Lewington.

Dad had been only 5 when the Second World War started and he was evacuated for nine months, as the family lived in the thick of things in Battersea, London. He ended up in Liss, Hampshire staying in four different billets. He didn't enjoy his time with any of them probably because he was so young and so missed his mum too much, and nothing really happened anyway as it was the period called 'the phoney war'. Therefore he went back to his family home and during that stay before the next evacuation, there was a massive explosion, which he has told me about. He says that it felt as though the whole house lifted off the floor, it was that loud. Plaster came off the walls, cracks appeared in the ceiling and he remembers the look of sheer terror on his mum's face. That bomb was 200 yards away and completely took out 3 entire streets and some railway lines. If the German's had dropped the bomb 200 yards in a different direction then I would certainly not be here now! Interestingly my dad has also had something published, an article about his time as an evacuee in the book 'The Day They Took the Children' by Ben Wicks, so writing runs in the family after all. Following this bombing - The Blitz - dad was evacuated again in 1943-44 this time to Carmarthenshire, South Wales. He stayed in a large mansion with the Lloyd family near Llangadog called Glansevin. He was 9 by this time and remembers this stay with fondness, as a period of adventure. Lots of children were forced to work but dad was one of the lucky ones. He returned to his mum in London after about 18 months when all had gone quiet again but as it turned out it was too early as it was just before the Germans sent down their doodlebugs (flying bombs).

Mum's Dad, Peter, was, of all things, a Fulham fan. He worked on the turnstiles at Fulham one week and Chelsea the next. So when dad met mum she was in fact a Fulham fan but it didn't take him long to convert her. Table tennis was a primary sport for both mum and dad (that's how they met) and they both loved watching football as well. Dad had in fact been a season ticket holder at Chelsea since 1962 after watching most games in the 50's by queuing up to buy tickets. He has also always loved watching cricket. Most recently both my parents have become keen bowls players although only mum competes. My cousin Ian was another important influence on me. He was a few years older than me and I always looked up to boys older than me as they were often stronger and better at sport. Ian and his family lived in Lightwater, and I used to cycle from Bagshot to see him. He had a large collection of Chelsea programmes in binders all neatly stacked in a bookcase. This inspired me to start my own collection and I now am the proud owner of every home programme issued since World War 2. As I am talking about inspirational figures, my major inspiration outside of my family was Ian Botham, the cricketing legend. Although football was my main sport, a perfect team activity just like cricket, I still thought of cricket from the perspective of a group of individual players, and Botham inspired me, so much so that I could not think of any other player. It really was a case of going to watch Botham rather than going to watch a cricket match.

When asked if I had a childhood dream, the only one which comes to mind is a desire to be a striker for Chelsea Football Club. Sport was and still is my life even though my relationship to it has changed over the years. Sport meant everything to me, as I was a good at it and it meant people looked up to me and respected me. It set me apart as someone special. My family background is a sporting one, as I have mentioned before; all of us have always been immersed in sport, and I grew up with that same passion which has never left me. I always loved football [Pics 26, 32 & 34], but I was good at all sports - cricket, table tennis, snooker, athletics. As a boy I could run

13

faster, jump higher and longer, hurdle faster and throw further than all my mates. Back then I had little time for anything else; all I wanted was to improve at everything I did. My parents were both keen table tennis players and both played at County level. When I played for Frimley, in the early 1980's, we entered a team as a family, my dad won 70% of his matches, mum won 50% of hers and I won 30% of mine. My great uncle, Harry Venner also represented England in the World Championships in 1950. Thirty years later as a young boy I became a table tennis champion at Butlins Bognor Regis. That's where I met an England International Table Tennis coach, who inspired me no end. [Pic 13]

Beyond my family, as a young boy my social networks were all based around school and more importantly sport, mainly football. Making friends back then was easy, it just happened. I have a clear memory of the first time I was picked for a team. One day at school, the games teacher, Mr Mothersole, watched a game we played and then began a process of picking his best two teams. He chose my friend Graham first, I had expected that he would pick me, but what hurt the most was when the teacher asked Graham to pick the first person to be in the opposing team, which meant because Graham wanted me to be on his team, he chose someone else, which to me meant I was thus judged the third best. This hurt a lot, an acute pain caused by my sporting ambition and the high standard I already set for myself in sporting achievement.

If I was not participating in sport with my friends I would be out during the summer riding my bicycle with them. We would meet up at the The Green, a large triangular area of grass. We would play football or cricket mostly, although we would be swept up with the nation's Wimbledon fever for two weeks as June turned to July, just like everyone else. Sport aside I would often sit with my mates on a green coloured telephone exchange box, which we would clamber onto, and talk for hours.

I had a full timetable of sporting activities as a young boy including: at least one football match every weekend and sometimes two; athletics meets during the summer; playing for Bagshot Cricket Club every Wednesday;

table tennis matches every Tuesday and practice on a Friday. I was fortunate to never be injured during a sport activity, only going to hospital once to get stitches for a cut in my head caused by a coat hook. This incident was as a result of a fight with another boy and actually looked much worse than it was - as usual with a cut to the head the blood was copious. However, by the age of 13 things did start to get very difficult for me as my disability began to raise its ugly head. I didn't know back then that this was the reason for my sporting prowess deserting me. I just thought like so many young sportsmen that my abilities had temporarily vanished. I did throw myself into snooker after this which continued for me until I reached the age of 20, when it became increasingly difficult to compete at the same level.

I have talked about being a good footballer but if truth be known I was on a par with many of my footballing peers, although my peers were all the good players of course. With table tennis it was a different story. I was the only one of my mates who played so it was a way for me to impress them. When they watched me play I felt special and this would in a strange way improve my game. The first memory I have of being a special sportsman is when I played in the Ballroom at Butlins which was set up with just one table tennis table and I played an exhibition match with the International Table Tennis coach, I have mentioned before. There were hundreds of people watching and I played the best table tennis of my life and the high I was on lasted for the rest of the week. I was only eleven years of age. Being good at sports meant I was respected and looked up to and it also made people want to be my friend. Sport had a powerful and positive effect on my self-esteem, although I think like a lot of kids what people thought of me didn't much matter. I had a lot of friends at school through my sporting activities and cannot remember ever falling out with any of them or having crossed words.

It was important to me for my parents to be proud of me, although another part of me maintained that it didn't much matter what people thought. We all carry this type of contradiction because nothing in life is perfect. I am sure they were proud of me, although they never said it. Being a good sportsman would be of particular significance to them, and would give the family a strong focus for discussion and ambition. In fact I suppose that my parents invested a lot of hope in my future as a sportsman. When my disability began to show itself, neither my parents nor I, as I have mentioned before, knew this was the reason for my sporting prowess deserting me. Despite what was to become a permanent loss of my skills, sport has always remained a major part of all the family's life even though I have no involvement in anything but watching it now, as I said before. It binds us together I think. It is a focal point, you might say.

Chapter 2.
Then and Now.

For a few years in my late teens and early twenties I wrote a diary every day, which I still have and which has formed the greater inspiration for this book. I no longer write one but I have for the purposes of explaining my life to viewers of my website and for readers of this book, written about various activities I attend and processes I have to follow in my life now. This chapter focuses on two diary entries [in italics] with a 24 year gap between them and describes the differences in my life then and now. It may be interesting to note I was 18 years old at the time of the first entry.

'Thursday 4th June 1987 - Yesterday I got up at 7.15am and took dad to Heathrow Airport. I went wrong on the way back but soon discovered so and corrected myself. I got home on time to take mum to work though. After this it was time to take Louise to school. The traffic at this time of day, on the A30, was terrible. It took me over half an hour to get there and back and that doesn't include the time I spent putting another £5 worth of petrol in the tank. At 12.45 I picked mum up from work and at 1.15pm I left to see nan and grandad. Nan made me lunch and then I had an appointment at Camberley Careers Office at 4.15pm. The lady at the Careers Office was very helpful, she took down notes of what I was interested in and I even told her about my disease in case she thought it may be a disadvantage for me in finding a job. She had no problem with this and she said it would not be a problem. I left at about 5.15. This evening I gave Gary a game of snooker, I played better than I had done for a week or two and I thrashed him 4-1. The only frame he did win was the second one and even then he fluked the deciding shot. I played really well - everything went in - it was amazing and maybe it will help me regain my appetite for snooker. A couple of weeks ago I had played Lee and I did not play well at all, after losing the first frame I became quickly disillusioned and even being ahead in the second with 4 or 5 reds remaining I still felt negative and thought I would lose it, which I did. In the 3rd frame I tried to forget about the first 2 and it seemed to be paying off as I led by 20 points with only two reds and the colours remaining.' But,*

Lee took the last 2 reds with blues and I eventually lost on the pink. It was not meant for me to win that day but today was very different. I was very pleased with myself. Afterwards I took Gary home and then went home myself and waited for dad to call so I could go and pick him up from Heathrow again.'

This entry above is from 1987 and is so short in comparison to the up to date one, seen later in this chapter, although this could be something to do with my youth and inexperience as a diarist of course, but for me it shows just how normal my everyday functioning was, and therefore not even worth mentioning. The difference between this entry and the one featured later and detailing a typical day now, is I suppose, that most people would not mention the fact that they have successfully made a cup of tea or got themselves up from bed and started their day, at least not in any great detail. The fact that back then in 1987 I could do most daily tasks with little or no fuss, removed the need to record every minute detail. Having said all this, I was functioning much better back in 1987 which meant I could live a busy lifestyle, doing all the things that one might expect of a young man, though I already had the disease in its early stages. However, when I now look back in my old diary I, like everyone else I suppose, had many days when nothing happened or when I was feeling not so good. It also strikes me that unlike now with my team of PA's supporting me to live my life, I actually was back in 1987 the one who supported all the family to live their lives. Back then I had a great deal of independence and autonomy despite my illness, which made all those things so much more possible. For example, the subsequent typing of a typical day, prior to commencing the writing of this book, took me two hours to type what had taken me 15 minutes to write freehand.

'Tuesday 5th April 2011- Jess, my PA has just left. We've done little today because I had arranged an Archery Introduction shoot this morning with the bowman of Warfield over in a field in Binfield (near Bracknell). This morning was wet, overcast and chilly but, I was nevertheless gearing up to go. However as I was about to make my 'Oat-so-Simple' for breakfast at 9.15 this morning, I got a phone-call from him [Rob Anderson] to ask if I was still coming. He told me the conditions were not ideal for Archery and that we

should try again next week at the same time. Chelsea are playing Man United away in the 2nd Leg of the Champions League Quarter-final that day but although very keen to go, Man United only gave Chelsea an allocation of 5 wheelchair tickets for the game (in a stadium that holds 78,000). I am not classed as one of the top 5 loyal wheelchair supporters in the club so was unable to get a ticket. So it's archery that day instead of a 4 hour drive up north!

Anyway, I digress. So me and Jess were indoors instead. She arrives at 9.30 on Tuesdays and so I set my alarm half an hour earlier to be up and ready for when she arrived. My morning routine today was: Alarm [Radio 2 comes on] at 7.30. I went to the bathroom, went to the toilet, got washed, cleaned my teeth, and shaved which took me up to 8.00.

I need help to dress in the mornings and at the moment this help comes from a device called a leg lifter. As I can't lift my right leg high enough to be able to grab it and place it by my left knee I use the leg lifter to do this. A leg lifter is simply a stick with a soft hook on the end in which to put my foot so I can pull it (with my hands). I then rest my foot on my left knee while I put my right sock on and while it's there I put my foot through the right leg hole of my underpants. I then repeat the process for my left leg using my right knee. Only this time I can lift my left leg high enough to be able to grab it with my right hand to place it on my right knee. Hence I don't need the leg lifter.

I then repeat the whole leg lifting process to put on my trousers until I am sitting in my wheelchair with just socks on and pants and trousers round my knees. My shirt goes on next which is quite simple but I must always concentrate on maintaining balance during this process of dressing. Time for my shoes next; again the leg lifting process has to start up but this time its easier as I already have my trousers on so I can use them to grab hold of, when lifting my leg up. My shoes are more like trainers really with Velcro straps and no laces for obvious reasons.

The next thing to do is attach the footrests to my chair. These are the parts of the wheelchair that your feet sit on all day. I take them off when I go to bed as otherwise they get in the way when transferring to the bed. I leave them off when I go into the bathroom in the mornings too as they get in the way transferring whilst naked to the toilet. "Why sleep naked?" I hear you ask. Well, would you want to go through that whole leg lifting process every night as well as every morning? Back to the footrests - they also don't allow me to get close enough to the sink to clean my teeth properly. So I leave them off until I am dressed.

When I clip on these footrests I can use them to press down on with my feet and lift my bum from my wheelchair for the few seconds required to slip my pants and trousers under to enable me to complete the 'getting dressed' routine. It's now 8.45.

I then go into the living room, I open the curtains (I have an extended pulley on both curtains to enable me to reach from my chair, [of which more later], I open the kitchen blind too (ditto the pulley), and place yesterday's washing from my lap (picked up from my bedroom floor 10 minutes earlier) in the machine. I then feed Zola, the cat. I set myself up first with a lap tray, they are so bloody useful these things, and help me to manage such small scale tasks. I keep her food bowl tucked under a work surface in the kitchen. I use a "Helping Hand Gripper" to grab the dish, drag it along the floor, reach down, pick it up, add a sachet of cat food and replace it using the same method. After this I wheel over to the computer, turn it and the TV on, and open the blind by my desk.

After my phone call from the Archery Centre today I had my breakfast and Jess arrived. I employ Jess for 5 hours (from 9.30 - 2.30 on Tuesdays). I like Jess. I feel we get on well and enjoy each-other's company.

So that explains where all my mornings go! At 10 O'clock I stood up in my frame for half an hour. I prefer to do this when Jess is here as it is somewhat physically challenging to maintain my balance while securing the strap behind me. We then watched part 3 of an ongoing documentary about Lilly

Allen's attempt at starting up a clothing sales and hire business with her sister. This continued until well after I had sat down.

I then started to think about dinner. My shopping was delivered yesterday by Tesco. I shop online every Sunday and last Sunday I had ordered 12 pork sausages so we decided to fry them up and have them with beans and mash. It was only then that I realised we had no potatoes. This is where having a PA is so beneficial for me. We agreed to pop down the road to buy some potatoes from the local supermarket in Lightwater Square. This is something I just would not do if I was on my own.

I put my jumper on, put my bum bag round my waist and wheeled into my bedroom. That's where I keep my powerchair. I removed the leg-rests from the chair in which I was sitting and using the 'floor to ceiling pole' by my television, I raised myself up, twisted and sat in the powerchair.

I can still drive my car but when a PA is with me it is far quicker to let them drive. So Jess drove the car today and I just wheeled up the ramp at the back of the vehicle and 'clicked' the powerchair into the floor. Jess passed me the seatbelt and I pulled it around me and handed it back to her. She then secured it by clicking it into its holder. This process only took a matter of seconds. I waited for Jess to step out the car and then closed the ramp and tailgate. A remote control that I keep attached to my powerchair opens the tailgate and lowers the ramp at the back of my car but when I'm in the car I can use the toggle switches located a reachable distance from me when sat in my chair. We set off and the journey took no more than 5 minutes and we parked in the car park situated just behind the supermarket. Jess first released the seat-belt and I released the chair from its lock on the floor and reversed down the ramp. Once out of the car, I raised the ramp and shut the tailgate with the remote control.

It is interesting to see how different the focus is in these two diary excerpts. Given the progress of my disease I now adapt my time accordingly, and as you can see there is much more involved in my daily routine, so it is impossible to fit so much into one day. The second diary entry speaks about outdoor activities in the briefest of details, with the majority of the entry focussing on the minute details of my day. Even though things take me longer each day, I am in fact a much more active and happy person, but rather like my day back in 1987 I do have some days when I am very busy and then others where I recuperate and rest. Both entries are just snapshots of my life on each day.

Since my diagnosis of ataxia I have managed to maintain my independence and this has been made possible in part by my indomitable spirit and determination to be self-reliant as much as I can be. I definitely think my life started when I got my proper diagnosis and decided to become a wheelchair user. Every positive aspect about my life today emanates from those two things. I am the same person with the same things that excite me and the same dreams I have always had but how different my life has become, with far more planning needed given the time it takes me to do stuff.

I struggled for years in the 1980's both supporting myself on furniture or using crutches which limited my functioning and also denying that something might be wrong with my body, but with my diagnosis it felt like I could finally be honest with myself and sort my life out for the better. In the second diary entry my wheelchair can be seen to be a positive part of me and my life rather than something to be scared of or anxious about. I spent so many years before the diagnosis just muddling along and yet unable to do so many things which I now take for granted.

Before, I had held a stereotypical view and I suspect one held by most people that having to start using a wheelchair is a negative step. When I was first diagnosed with ataxia I went to see a physiotherapist, Sue Edwards, at The National Hospital for Neurology and Neurosurgery in Queen Square, London for advice on a daily physio routine to adopt. I spoke to her about my fears in starting to use a wheelchair. She told me I may feel a bit negative about having to use one "But," she said, "Don't think of it as having a negative effect on your life but instead of it having an empowering effect on your life. Life can be better for you now, because you can start to organise all aspects of your life to support you to live a much better one" This was a revelation to me and I still feel so positive about it to this day. I can now see how right she was. By admitting that I had a disability and that I needed a wheelchair for my own safety and overall health, I realised that I could have a better life with increased public and personal support for me and for my condition. Now my wheelchair enables me to do so many things which would not have been possible before.

When I look back I can see just exactly how much things have changed for me. However, I have successfully met every challenge that life and my ataxia has thrown at me, and I know that I will continue to do so. A positive attitude is the thing that has always got me through, I have never viewed any challenge as a problem, and therefore it has been possible to make a real and positive difference to my life, my independence and my happiness, through using my brain and my determination to make the necessary changes.

Chapter 3.
My Driving.

In those days of my youth, before parents were 'duty bound' to provide their offspring with a car each and as I had no work, and therefore no money of my own, you can imagine my frustration at not having my own transport. This frustration was highlighted as I watched, over time my mates all get their own vehicles, some very smart too, like Neal who had just got a Triumph Spitfire, a very nice car, which only served to remind me just how much I wanted one. So I was caught in a double dilemma, both needing a car to improve my quality of life alongside my developing disability (not that I knew it was developing at the time) and not having a vehicle which in itself might improve my chances of employment. In those unenlightened days before the Disability Discrimination Act (1995), having a disability made it less likely to be considered for long-term employment and even after the Act's passing it was still an uphill battle for disabled people to challenge an organisation who discriminated or who refused to consider reasonable adjustments to enable a disabled person to access work and the workplace.

Having passed my driving test in 1987 the scene was set in my mind for the introduction of a car into my life. This was definitely for me a great step forward. I passed at the fourth attempt and must say I was surprised to have passed even then.

'This good news was soon overshadowed by a letter that I received from the DVLA which stated that they had received information suggesting I may not be fit to continue to drive safely, because of my legs. This information had obviously come from the driving examiner and could only have been based on the answers I gave him on my test when he asked about my 'wobbly walking'. Thus began a difficult time, of waiting for a decision from them once they had received my completed medical form. At the same time I wrote to my consultant, Dr. Lee, to inform him that I would for the time being continue to drive until the investigations were completed and I had a result either way. I was determined to appeal a negative decision though as having a car had become my lifeblood. This as you can imagine was extremely frustrating and raised in me such a feeling of injustice. I thought to myself -

'Why can't I be like everyone else and just be given an ordinary license, I passed my test fair and square.'

Hurrah! A matter of weeks later my own license arrived. I could tell immediately that it was my license as the letter visible through the window of the envelope was pink. The summary of entitlement on the license said 'restricted' but all this means is that I couldn't drive heavy goods vehicles, which I had no desire to do anyway. So I had become a fully licensed driver and I was very happy about that.

'Yesterday is a day I will probably never forget - the one on which I passed my driving test'

Even when I passed my driving test the 'problem of my legs' came up, and try as I might I could not help but be upset by the examiners reference to it during my test. A mere month later though I was stunned to receive a letter from my consultant Dr Lee at Frimley Park Hospital. He said he had received a letter from Dr Patten (the neurologist at Royal Surrey Hospital, Guildford) telling him of my problem - a lack of coordination in my legs, as he called it. He wanted to see me the next day to discuss my driving ability. Thank heavens I did not have to wait long for the appointment, I spent the evening worrying in desperation at the prospect of having my license taken away from me after so much effort on my part to pass the test and having subsequently realised the vital importance to me, of being able to drive myself. I am not joking when I say that if my license was to be taken away then I would've topped myself. So the next day I went to see Dr Lee but instead was seen by a locum doctor in his place. I tried to persuade him to support me in keeping my license and he said 'You must never focus on things you can't do, think only about what you CAN do?' I was expecting a rough ride but this was the first doctor who believed in me and made me realise that thinking negatively was no good if I wanted to keep my license. I told him about my driving, and the need to keep going, not least for my future employment which I would not be able to get to without a car. Thankfully, the result of this discussion and the previous one was that both Dr Lee and this locum doctor seemed just to trust that I knew my capabilities.

The other problem I had faced since before my efforts to pass my test was the fact that my parents to which I have alluded at the opening of this chapter had told me in no uncertain terms that I can have a car only when I start working which is fair enough, but that would mean I wouldn't have one to drive to work on my first day, so how would I get there? My horror at this, given that it was most likely that my grandad would be the one to drive me to my first day of work, was the height of my 'finding work' teenage worries. In the time after my license arrived and the fateful letter from Dr Lee mentioned above I was to drive only the family car becoming a family taxi driver. One exciting happening which soon however, turned awry was, when my dad took the car in to be repaired and hired instead a lovely D registration, sparkling White Escort 1.3 L. It looked lovely to drive and I hastily planned out my week... Tuesday I would take Andrew to snooker, on Wednesday I could take mum to work and then take the car to school and even take it to Camberley, later. I was already using the family car to take mum to work, Louise to the stables where she was working for a few weeks and even dropping off dad at the airport. Having become the family's taxi driver I assumed that I would get a chance to drive the new flash motor. However, all this was too good to be true, as dad told me that no one under 25 years of age could drive a hire car. Why, why could he not have told me earlier on? Instead he allowed me to build up my hopes and plan my week. I was bloody annoyed, it would have been a chance to impress my peers and who knows even a few girls.

Having a car, for me, of course meant having an ability to get to work and to help my family, of which more later, but if I am honest even more so it meant being able to have a chance to get a girlfriend - my major dream in life and one as yet unfulfilled - for anything more than six months anyway. I assumed, as so many teenage boys do, that a car was a magnet for the girls, and the fact that I didn't have my own car, (and it seemed even in the short or medium term I would not get one) filled me with a deep depression. How was I to make any kind of impression if I could not give a girlfriend a lift home or to work, or take her out to the cinema?

'I feel so immobile without a car - it seems that I am glued to the house without one. If I do not get one for my birthday I will buy one. It is as simple as that.'

So you see my parent's decision to block my having a car before I was in work was actually totally hampering my ability to both get work and find a woman. On top of that shortly after my driving test and the arrival of my license my mum and dad announced that they were thinking of spending £3700 on new windows. Looking back I can see how that was a good idea and of course they were entitled to use their money as they saw fit, but at the time I could not believe how windows might be more important than a new 'top of the range stereo and more importantly a car for me. Surely, I thought, a car for me is much more important than some bloody windows and would be over £3000 cheaper. All I could think in my disbelief was that they had already secretly bought me a car for my birthday; after all you could get a reasonable one back then for £500.

Give my dad his due it was not long before he bought a new car, a mark IV escort, but it seemed strange and was difficult to drive. It was a car for his work of course, so would be unavailable for me to drive during the week.

'The real and cruel twist here is that I have a car parked outside, something I am pleased about, but it is not mine of course which is the important point, and therefore I have nowhere to drive and am unable to make any plans. Having a car of my own makes it easy to choose where to go and to organise

my life as I wish. In this situation I have no chance of having a girlfriend waiting for me to pick her up, as my mates do, they all have cars of their own and therefore much more street credibility.'

Some months later whilst working as a volunteer at a summer sports activity centre I had met a girl called Andrea, and as I had the family car for this work, I dreamed of seeing more of her and of being able to take her to places. This was the case for as long as our relationship lasted and I had total responsibility for the car for two weeks as mum and dad were away on holiday. As the time for their return drew nearer, I realised that although I wanted to see them it would also mean giving up the car. I had enjoyed the last two weeks and loved the independence. I knew I would feel stuck to the house without it and would soon start to find myself getting very bored. I was sure I had to have a car of my own or a job or preferably both. Without anything to do I'd start getting depressed and I already knew that that is one of the worst feelings in the world and as I'd been feeling good for over a month, this was a bitter blow.

To cap it all, an unfortunate event occurred which typically damaged my standing with my dad. I'd had no problem driving alone whilst they were away for two weeks but now they were back, dad once again insisted on accompanying me when I used his car. Fair enough I guess. One evening I went to snooker in Camberley, and I dropped dad off at a friend's, close to the club on the way. I was thus on my own and I parked in a different place than usual. I knew as soon as I put it there I would have problems getting out and so it proved. I met dad at the car for our return journey and I was hoping that dad would drive but when I asked him he said he'd been driving for a long time that day so I took the wheel. Dad was in the car with me for the first time in two weeks today so I was keen to repay the trust he put in me. I reversed out slowly, just squeezing past a parked car. Dad said "You were a bit close their son" to which I replied "Close enough" and then as I moved off, I just scraped the side of our car on the rear corner of the parked one. You could just hear the scrape. Bloody typical! Two weeks without as much as a touch and then this. I felt so small I just wanted to disappear into the chair. Once I had passed my test I always did hate driving with dad in the car and now even more so. I made a decision in fact not to ever drive his car with him in it again.

During these weeks I hoped against hope that a car would appear. I wouldn't care what it was. A Fiesta or Escort would be nice but I would even settle for grandad's Ital, and that is saying something! I would think to myself, is it too much to ask for? Anyway, where would my parents get the money from? Maybe they do not intend to buy a new TV and new windows, maybe they have been saving up the money to buy me a car. I know now that if I had spoken to my parents then I could have stopped mulling these thoughts over in my mind. Instead I used to get very upset about lots of these sort of things that were on my mind and I often couldn't hold myself together. I was in fact depressed every day, a feeling totally gone now, but back then it was a desperate time for me. The end of my independence occasioned by the loss of the sole use of a car was the main factor and not having a job made this worse with the possibility of getting one as remote as ever.

One thing became clear on my birthday though; I had not got a car for my present, but I knew that was more hope than belief anyway. In the meantime following my parents return from holiday, I had seen the careers officer and they suggested seeing the disablement officer at the jobcentre. It sounded frightening at first, but they may help put me in the picture a bit. I couldn't go the next day as I didn't have the car. I told mum and dad that it was no good waiting to get a job before I got a car. I needed one right then. They actually understood how I felt and said they would talk to grandad about the possibility of him selling his. Disappointment again! (His Morris Ital) but at least it was a set of wheels. Finally it looked as though grandad was not selling his car just yet. I was gutted as I desperately needed a car 'now'. I could not live my life to the full without one and I felt everyone should be able to live their life to the full.

I guess the family may have been talking in depth about my predicament because I did not have long to wait to get the news for which I had been waiting so long. Suddenly the position with the car completely changed as Grandad wanted to buy a new one and he said that the family could buy his for £800. It seemed also that mum and dad had more than enough money in an account that I knew nothing about and they said that I needn't pay anything. What a result! The car had five months tax left on it and all that was needed was the insurance. It was to be a family car with family insurance and was to be ours very soon maybe after nan and grandad's cruise. My first motor was to be a manual Ital then, not exactly a fashionable car but it had been 100% reliable and looked after since it was bought in 1981.

Grandad and mum sorted out the insurance, and the insurance company did not look at my license. This was just as well because if they had they would have seen it carrying restrictions and therefore it may have cost us more. Like so many new cars it seemed a bit awkward to start with as its long floppy gear stick made quick gear changes seem impossible. But I got more used to it the more I drove it and with a cassette player in it and the Chelsea sticker in the back, I was sure it would be fine. I started from then on to take friends up to the snooker club in the Ital. Over time though I began to get very uncomfortable driving as I nearly hit two cars when I took my friend Lee to snooker one evening. This feeling was not helped by the fact that the Ital had some developing technical problems. It was awful to drive when it was cold and also the left indicator didn't work sometimes, and the ignition only worked when it felt like it. I was once stuck at the garage for 10 minutes trying to start the bloody thing. It was so embarrassing! However, despite the problems with the Ital, soon afterwards and for the first time, I did a long journey in it to go and see Phil Collins at Wembley. I used my 'disabled badge' to get as close to the entrance as possible. Using the badge felt totally foreign to me but it was much needed as it would otherwise have been a real struggle for me to get from the car to the arena entrance.

Now that I had the motor sorted I turned my attention to both work and the pursuit of a relationship. Thinking about these things could still evoke a depression which in turn was remedied by going out in my car and driving round and round, up and down, nowhere in particular. I just drove. I was almost hoping for a fatal accident as I drove around and if that's not been suicidal again what is? I was still feeling I would rather be dead than in this predicament. In November 1987 I almost got my wish, when I crashed the car, which resulted in the most difficult six months as I waited for the case to go to court. On a drive to Aldershot, when approaching a set of traffic lights they turned amber, I made a split second decision to drive across them rather than screech to a halt. I then collided with a car that had jumped her red light when she saw mine change to amber. A couple of hundred yards behind, on his motorcycle, a policeman had seen the whole incident and his statement (so I found out a few weeks later) stated that I had jumped the red light. His word would have been believed above an 18 year old boys so my dad advised me to just plead guilty and take my punishment.

Even once the case was cleared up, with a three point endorsement and £100 fine, I still had to attend a meeting with Dr Lee, my consultant to discuss the fact that I may be a risk to myself and other drivers. I worried desperately that my disability might get me into further trouble. My solicitor was not very reassuring leading up to the trial. He had dealt with many people with disabilities before though not someone with Charcot-Marie Tooth Disease. It was he who had said to plead, not in person but by post, as my disability if seen and commented upon by the magistrate could result in prejudicial treatment against me and may even impact on my ability to hold a license in the future. This as I have said before, would have been devastating. In a nutshell I didn't see how I was driving without due care and attention. Okay, so I may have gone through an amber light. I did not see a red light. But witnesses (the policeman) had said the lights were red when I went through. The court is bound to take witness's words and not mine. However, in my opinion I did the safest thing, I did not jam on the brakes. The only thing that would count against me is that I could well have been speeding. I cannot be sure, but 30 mph is very slow. Besides the damage to the cars proved I was going faster than 30 apparently. So bang to rights I guess. A Policeman's testimony may have sealed my fate.

In late 1987 after my accident in the Ital, I bought a second car - a Ford Fiesta. It was red with a fawn roof. This belonged to friends of my parents. Fiestas are one of my favourite type of cars and this was a car I could take pride in. Not that I didn't take pride in the Ital, it's just that the Fiestas are more suited to teenagers. Even after 26 years I can still remember the registration number - KCD 587W. They were selling it for £1500. This is slightly more than we were going to pay but grandad had said he would pay £300 and I said I would pay £200 so mum and dad would pay the remaining £1000. It was a lot of money, but again we had a history of the car and it was a car I could be proud of and feel good about being seen in.

'I have driven the car already today and although I felt quite comfortable and drove it okay, I did find that the accelerator was a bit high off the floor. In moving the seat back I had solved that problem only to come up against another one, clutch now being too far away resulting in missing gear changes sometimes. Still, you can't win them all!'

A month before my court case came up for the original accident I had another crash, this time in the Fiesta. This time it was entirely my fault. The traffic was moving very slowly, 25 mph approximately down Jenkins Hill. It then speeded up and so did I. I put the car into third gear and accelerated to about 30 or 35 mph, still quite slow. When I looked up the car in front was braking. There was plenty of time to do likewise, or there seemed to be but instead of pushing down the brake pedal I hit the accelerator. The car in front got closer to me as my speed increased, it was a frightening position to be in. I then hit the brake. The tyres screeched and then bang. I just sat there. I couldn't believe it. It had to be a bad dream but I didn't wake up. I could not have felt lower as I sat there. I got out and looked at the damage - hers was worse than mine. She also hit the car in front of her (a BMW). I had a look at that but I could see no damage. My bumper was dented and liquid was leaking out of the engine. We exchanged addresses and although she advised me to call the AA, I drove straight off with no trouble, as did she and the bloke in front of her.

'I still feel nervous when I think about the crash. I still can't believe it happened. One second, I'm happily driving along the road, the next I'm skidding towards the back of another car.'

It had happened and there was nothing I could do. I wished I could go back in time and begin the journey home again but it was no dream as I said before - I had to just get on with it. Now I was car-less again, my dad insisting that the Fiesta should go into the garage to be checked over. My independence was temporarily gone again. It was soon to go for a longer period as my dad needed a car again now that he had a new job, so my Fiesta fitted the bill exactly. Damn!

As my disability progressed over the years I needed further adaptations in order to a) make life easier and b) ensure my ongoing independence. This has necessitated at each purchase a sharp learning curve as I sought to appraise myself of the various ways that not only each vehicle was designed, as everyone does, but also the various adaptations. Most people never have to face a different way of driving or entering a vehicle but for me it was like learning from scratch each time and for which I never received training.

So far I had had two cars bought privately and without the assistance soon to be due to me because of my disability. In 1991 I got my first 'Motability' car - a Peugeot 205 Automatic. It was my parents who first mentioned the 'Motability' scheme to me because I think I still was in 'denial' about being disabled at all. Before, their advice would have fallen on deaf ears. However, there was no other way of getting a brand new car so I went along with it. I bought it on hire purchase for 2 reasons 1- It was then mine to sell after 5 years and I could keep the money!! and 2- As in effect it became mine from day one, I had the freedom to 'personalise it'. This I did shortly after getting it by adding a black spoiler across the back window and a red stripe all-round the bodywork also. I felt like the 'bees knees' behind the steering wheel. I loved driving it and being seen in it.

Having had my ataxia diagnosis in January 1993, I decided 3 months later to approach the council about moving into my own flat. 7 months later, once this had been approved I moved in and at that time I began to use a wheelchair almost full time. In 1995 I really felt a wheelchair was necessary at work too. The civil service welfare people arranged this for me and I felt much happier using a wheelchair (I was no longer fearful about falling over whenever I left my desk). However I still used crutches between the office door and the car and then the car and my front door when I got home.

To make my life easier and to assist me with my poor balance I arranged to have a handrail fitted to the bodywork of my car, between the driver's side front and rear windows. This made it far easier to balance myself when unlocking the door with the key. Back then of course there was no remote 'unlock' button on the key, or at least not on basic car models which mine was. This of course meant drilling into the bodywork of the car thus devaluing it and making it look rather odd. It had to be done though as my worsening balance was affecting my ability to find the keyhole of the door. It gave me somewhere to lean my crutches too as I needed a free hand to get the key in the lock and the other hand gripping the rail so as not to fall over. It also made it easier for me to throw both crutches into the back of the car as I could grab hold of this handrail with my non-throwing hand.

This 'part-time wheelchair dependence' became physically and mentally more and more difficult to cope with (I was becoming fearful of falling when using crutches to cover even these short distances). Eventually Social Services awarded me some limited support at each end of the day to get me from the house to the car in the morning and from the car to the house in the evening. I had to find a way of using the wheelchair between car and house/office. My friend and colleague John Ebbs used to bring out the chair from the office for me and take it back in when I left. The answer was a rooftop hoist so I could take the chair around with me all the time (and I then had a choice of wheelchairs as I needed to use only one all the time and not use different ones at home and in the office).

My next car was a Renault Clio Auto which I got in 1996, it came with a rooftop hoist fitted to it. This was called a GZ91 wheelchair stowing hoist and was fitted by Cowal Mobility Aids in High Wycombe. (A drive back from High Wycombe became a regular 'first drive in my new car' for each of 4 cars). Over time driving this car safely became a problem though. Due to increasing co-ordination problems in my legs I began using my right foot for the accelerator and my left foot for the brake as this meant no coordination was needed. But I realised this was not the right way to drive when Lee followed me one day and told me my brake light was on all the time. I realised my foot must have been touching the brake pedal and not merely hovering over it. The prospect of another accident became very real if I continued to drive in this way. I had a driving assessment at MAVIS (Mobility Advice and Vehicle Information Service) at Crowthorne and they tested me using 'push, pull' hand controls. This one trial made me realise this was the answer. There followed a difficult month of driving knowing I wasn't driving safely while waiting for the hand controls to be funded and paid for. I had them fitted by a Renault dealer in Ascot. This Motability accredited dealership was later closed by Motability when they discovered customers were being advised (for no reason) to have bodywork repaired in their bodywork garage, where fraudulent insurance claims were being made.

Motability has to give training now, but back then they didn't for me, other than the short trial at MAVIS I was in at the deep end, with no instruction. Did I need to push or pull the lever which stuck out from the steering wheel to brake? I remember as I approached the first road junction with my new hand controls I pushed the lever down just to see what would happen. As it happened the brakes came on. Within two weeks however I had become totally familiar and more than comfortable using hand controls. Driving became a pleasure rather than a worry again.

I had two further cars, a Renault Clio and a Ford Focus within the next six years both obtained through Motability and both with hand controls and rooftop hoists. But in the latter part of 2005, having just got a Motability Ford Fusion, another mobility problem became apparent. Due to the degenerative nature of my disability it was becoming too difficult for me to stow the wheelchair in the GZ91 hoist. I was finding it was taking too much out of me. It was exhausting for me. In 2005 I was also beginning to see the benefits of using a powerchair. I had been using a mobility scooter for a good few years before then and enjoyed the freedom that gave me. It enabled me to get away from my house and just go off down the road. This sounds like a straightforward activity but for me I had never been able to do that before. It was lovely to just get out in the sun and actually meet people! However, a mobility scooter makes it impossible to get in and out of small shops and so became rather frustrating. Darren also moved to the neighbourhood in 2004 (he has Muscular Dystrophy and uses a powerchair). I remember I used to see him out and about and I thought 'I'd like a bit of that'. It was he who had seen the 'internal transfer WAV' at a mobility roadshow. He said I should take a look online. I did and I knew this was a way of solving all the problems above.

So I bought a powerchair and set the wheels in motion to get a Wheelchair Accessible Vehicle (WAV). I finally ended the contract on the Ford Fusion early. It had become just too difficult to fold the chair outside the car and maintain my balance whilst seated on the driver's seat with my legs outside the car. I just couldn't do it anymore. In addition to this, I figured it might speed Motability up with my WAV application if I had no Motability vehicle at all. Between making my mind up that a WAV was the solution to my needs and actually getting it was a very difficult period. I got so frustrated with Motability's delays that I even wrote to my MP to complain. I won't bore you with the 'whys and wherefores' but needless to say, soon after, I received the vehicle. The whole process took 1 Year, 3 months & 6 days after application to come to fruition.

So I finally got the Renault Kangoo WAV on a five year lease. The adaptions were funded by Motability Grants Department. I got this car on 3rd November 2006, it was my 6th Motability car and was the first that I had been able to use with my powerchair. I had it for 5 years and a few months. It varied from a standard car in the following ways:

1. Hand controls: This is a push/pull lever situated just behind the steering wheel which is connected directly to the ordinary feet controls. This enables me to use the accelerator pedal by pulling the lever towards me and the brake pedal by pushing the lever away from me... This was the 5th car I had with hand controls fitted. The push/pull lever also has an indicator toggle and a beam toggle fitted to it to enable me to signal and shine the beam without taking my hand off it.

2. Automatic tailgate and ramp: This enables me to enter the vehicle in my powerchair and thus take my powerchair around with me. I have a remote control which has 4 buttons on it: Tailgate open, Ramp out, ramp in and Tailgate close. I use buttons 1 & 2 when approaching the car to enter it and buttons 3 & 4 after exiting. When inside the car I can use a further 2 toggle switches that perform the same 4 tasks. These toggle switches are located close to where I park my chair.

3. Wheelchair locking device: This enables me to automatically lock my powerchair to the floor of the car. I can do this by simply positioning the chair in the correct place. The car was totally adapted by a company called Aspect Conversions, they have since gone bust. They took my powerchair for a few days shortly before I took delivery of the car. This was so that they could attach a pin to the bottom of the chair that fits perfectly inside the lock on the floor of my car. The chair is thus locked securely in the car and meets all health and safety requirements. I can also be driven whilst sitting in my powerchair in this position, again this complies with health and safety regulations so long as I'm wearing the seatbelt. The device is unlocked by pressing another button close to where the chair is parked.

4. An automatic driver's seat (known as a Ricon 6 way power transfer seat): This enables me to transfer myself from my powerchair (in its lock) to the driver's seat and then to the driving position behind the steering wheel. The 6 movements of the seat are: back and forwards (as can be adjusted manually in normal cars), up and down & side to side. The car gave me total freedom and independence which would not have been possible without Motability's input.

Soon after getting the Kangoo, with its state of the art adaptations, I was driving down a road in Lightwater, a windy road as it happened, and I deliberately cut a corner off, I just couldn't be bothered to steer correctly round it, as there were no cars around, but as luck would have it an eagle-eyed policeman driving an unmarked police car 200 yards back had spotted this and when he'd caught me up, he stopped me! He detected my movement to be uncoordinated as I reached for and pressed the 'window down button' He looked into my eyes and said "have you been drinking? Could I ask you to get out of the car and walk in a straight line?" I explained that I had a disease called ataxia which would make that very difficult. In fact I could not walk. He looked in the back of the Kangoo and saw my wheelchair. Then he let me off, saying "Be careful when you are driving". It seems easy for the police and others to mistake ataxia for drunkenness, a fact which is now acknowledged through police training and public awareness-raising work.

The less people criticise my driving the better and maybe with my ataxia I am sure to get my fair share. I know my driving is not going to be as good as other people's, as my limbs are uncoordinated and don't move smoothly. However I am constantly assessing myself and my ability to drive safely, and when I begin to doubt myself and become nervous about my ability I will give up. I feel okay presently and in control and so I will keep driving. I judge myself based on other people who have ataxia, and virtually all others have given up by my age. I know I have a responsibility to other drivers and the DVLA. The DVLA are good enough to allow me to keep my license and to be honest with myself. I have no fear about carrying on at the moment. I don't drive more than three quarters of an hour at one time. Any more than that and I will arrange for a PA to drive the journey using the 'open policy' on my Motability insurance. Any PA can drive my car thanks to Social Services letting insurers know that I need PAs to drive my car for me. Anyone with my permission can drive for me, on my insurance as long as I have seen their driving licence.

One incident that I see as quite amusing was once whilst sat with my parents having driven myself round to their house, there was a knock at the door. It was the lady from next door to them telling us that the driver's side Kangoo door was wide open. I knew exactly what had happened but everyone else must have been slightly puzzled. I need light in the car to be able to exit out the back in my powerchair. The way of getting light is to open the driver's door so the internal light comes on. I need to reverse and twist the Ricon drivers' seat, transfer to the power chair, replace the right footplate on the chair, swivel and move forward the Ricon drivers' seat to enable me to reverse the power chair out at the right angle, release the powerchair from its lock, open the tailgate and drop the ramp and then reverse the powerchair down it. I need to be able to see what I'm doing in the dark! As the whole operation of getting out of my car takes 10 minutes + I think I can be forgiven for making the odd mistake by forgetting to close the driver's door!

When I'd had my Kangoo nearly 5 years I expected to get some sort of correspondence from Motability to tell me the lease was nearly up. That correspondence didn't come and via a telephone call to them I learned that the 5 year lease had been extended to a 7 year lease. I had set my heart on a new vehicle and had even pre-empted a change by selecting a new replacement and contacting the supplier (Sirus Automotive). It was a bit unfair of Motability to tell me that the lease had been extended at this late stage. Luckily in that time the family acquired some money. The advance payment for this new vehicle (A VW Caddy) was £14,000. With the adaptions I needed being a further £3,200. I would have to pay this money otherwise I would have had to have the Kangoo for another two years.

Quite a few things had gone wrong with the Kangoo by the end of its' 5th year. The wire to make the Ricon drivers' seat swivel split, and it stopped working totally, and before I'd swivelled round too. I had to ring my dad to help me get out my car on that occasion. The remote control I used to open the tailgate and drop the ramp failed and replacing the batteries made no difference. The Kangoo was supplied and converted by a company called 'Aspect Conversions' so they would have been the ideal people to report this to. Except of course Aspect Conversions were no longer around. Just after accepting money from disabled drivers for vehicles they never supplied! Motability managed to put me in touch with a company called Mountside Mobility who fixed all the problems. Motability picked up the bill. I got to know Mountside Mobility quite well during the 5th year of the lease.

My parents got together the money required for the Advance Payment for the VW Caddy and I found the money for the adaptations. After having my driving fully assessed at the Queen Elizabeth Foundation Mobility Service in

Carshalton, Surrey and a fitting (a period of time where Sirus Automotive have my powerchair in their workshop to get the fittings all correct) I took delivery of my new vehicle early in 2012. It is like my Kangoo in that it is an internal transfer vehicle but it is a class up and far more comfortable to drive. It's in Chelsea blue of course. Unlike the Kangoo it comes with a fob remote control. You press the button on the fob once and the vehicle drops by about 5 inches, the tailgate opens and the ramp lowers all automatically and in sequence.

Each major change I made in my cars was for the better. A change was an improvement, making it safer or easier. In the car I have now, the only change I would make would be not to transfer – i.e.: drive whilst sat in my wheelchair. The problem though is I have a lot people that drive for me, this would make it difficult for anyone to drive me as they would have no seat to drive from. In the past I used to only be driven to Chelsea games but as my condition has progressed people drive for me every day now to speed things up a bit.

I cannot say just how important my vehicles have been to me but the fact that I have been a Motability customer and they have always and continue to meet my needs in terms of adaptations to ensure I can remain independent and self-determining, is beyond praise. As you will see in other chapters of this book I continue to remain my own person and a member of my community, through the commitment of designers and funders and my own determination to achieve a balanced and ordinary life, paid for thanks to a windfall that my family had received.

Chapter 4.
My Travels.

As I have said earlier, ataxia began to make itself felt when I was aged around 13. The major symptom of the disease for me was my worsening ability to walk, which made it difficult to consider all but a few trips abroad and those were mostly single city visits. If I were able to get to a place but then remain there, then there was less chance of any access or mobility issues occurring. Who led this idea I am not certain. Perhaps it was my parents' reticence about the effect of foreign travel on me which prevented me travelling more. I think though, that it was more likely due to my own embarrassment about my 'struggle to walk', something I pretty soon could not do unaided. The few trips I was able to make abroad as a child and teenager included Paris, Perpignan in the south of France, Ibiza and Mallorca in Spain and a couple of trips to Amsterdam in Holland with my football club. For the most part, however family holidays included a regular visit to Butlins, at Bognor Regis which I loved because of the sports facilities there; I could still excel as a snooker player which was a good smokescreen for my progressive disability. In some ways, at least until later in my life, I had not even thought of myself as a traveller but perhaps more as a holidaymaker and of course a travelling sports fan.

One thing which helped me to recognise the possibility of enjoyable travel occurred before my diagnosis of ataxia at the age of 23. There was a work trip to Calais in France and for me it seemed an impossible thing to even consider with my crutches and my very real fear of falling over even when using them. A colleague at the time, Debbie Morson, suggested that work should rent a wheelchair for me. I was shocked to hear this suggestion at first but soon realised, as she had, that it was either this or remain in the office with everyone else out enjoying themselves. I had no option but to agree and - goodness what a revelation! For the first time I felt like one of the gang and was not called upon to explain my disability or face what had become an 'elephant in the room'. I had such fun. After this trip I felt at last that I may have found a way to overcome my embarrassment about walking

41

something which was destined to determine my future travel plans and ambitions.

Soon after the work trip and following the official diagnosis of ataxia on the 8th January 1993, I was being assessed at the National Hospital for a standing frame. At this time I was also being 'prescribed' my first wheelchair, a daunting prospect for me and one which made me feel as though I was giving up and giving in and consequently, to my former sportsman's eyes, somewhat of a failure. During this particular 'standing frame' assessment I had had the discussion mentioned earlier with Sue Edwards, my neurology physiotherapist about the use of a wheelchair. I had told her I couldn't help but think of the step to using one as anything but negative and restricting. She said "It will be an enabling device, think of the "world as your oyster" she said. These words impressed me and for the first time I realised that travel with all its challenges for any of us, may for me, actually be possible. How right she was! Before using a wheelchair, I considered any access problems as my own fault. Afterwards, I saw access problems as the fault of society in general, and with that in mind I realised that there is always a solution. Suddenly my mortifying discomfort about walking evaporated. If I did not need to try to walk but could instead change to being a wheelchair user then that self-consciousness would have no place in my life.

So - have wheels will travel? Well of course, it is not quite as easy as that. Being a wheelchair user opens up a whole load of issues relating to access which I did not face in the same way when I was walking with crutches. The major issue for me and one which impacts on me still and upon my personal comfort and dignity is 'where can I next go to the toilet?' There are two issues here: firstly how long will it be before I can reach the next toilet and secondly will I be able to use said toilet when I do? I, of course can minimise the former by making appropriate plans before I leave the house but sadly in the case of the latter it is still a lottery when thinking of accessibility, although I have to say things are much better nationally than they ever were before. To help with this worry I finally made an appointment in mid-2013 with a Uro-neurologist at the Hospital for Neurology and Neurosurgery in Queens Square to discuss these and other 'pee-problems'. I was advised to take a drug called Vesicare [solifenacin succinate]. This drug comes in tablet form and works by relaxing the involuntary muscle that is found in the wall of the bladder. I no longer have any urgency problems and I am now far less worried when being away from my own toilet.

With all the access issues in my mind and addressed as much as possible, I find the only real issue I have when travelling on the UK mainland is planning for and finding a PA to drive me wherever I want or need to go. I can still drive of course but never for more than half an hour or three quarters of an hour at a push at one time these days. In the UK I always have the alternative of remaining in my wheelchair and sitting in it whilst in my WAV (Wheelchair Accessible Vehicle). This I do for short journeys but it can be a little isolating, because hearing what the driver is saying above the noise of a fast engine, with the driver facing the other way is impossible for me. It is still just about possible for me to transfer myself from my wheelchair to the passenger seat of a car with the assistance of a PA for longer journeys. This makes me feel more involved: it is easier to talk to the driver and I have a clear view of the road ahead.

For a longer trip in the UK, planning involves the following: Ensuring I have enough money in my PA account to pay a PA; securing the services of a PA, someone to drive me somewhere and be there with me throughout my activity; until recently considering which of my 2 chairs to take, usually based on whether I am familiar with the surroundings when I get there. If am not familiar with the place where I am going, I would take my manual chair as I am generally more comfortable in this one and in more control of it; analysing the abilities and strengths of the chosen PA, when I needed to be pushed over distance in my manual chair I had to take these factors into account and weighing up the independence I would gain through using my slightly more cumbersome powerchair. So with this all in place I am ready for a trip anywhere on the UK mainland.

Going abroad is more of an issue as more often than not it involves longer periods of time, and so more money must be found to pay a PA. Most of my PA's have other jobs too, so finding someone with a spare week or even a few days can be troublesome. The possibility of travelling from home to anywhere abroad in the back of a WAV is also difficult as long distance driving is too exhausting and uncomfortable for me. I have yet to find a suitable WAV to hire abroad and anyway, a WAV would need to meet my particular needs. All London taxis are wheelchair accessible. You should be able to rent a vehicle like this for my PA to drive from any airport in the world. If only!

Airports don't give wheelchair users a particularly pleasant experience. I have found that boarding aeroplanes means being treated in a very undignified manner. My attitude is either 'grin or bear it' or don't fly - for me the choice is a simple one. Wheelchair users are forced to be transferred into a seat on the aircraft. This is not necessary. Wheelchairs could be clamped down firmly to the floor and seat-belts could be designed to securely hold the users in their chairs. Seat-belts need only be worn during take-off and landing so to me it is no big problem. It would save the need for an assistance crew at the airport and would speed up the time taken to board wheelchair passengers. Another boon would be a much more accessible toilet on planes.

A trip abroad becomes a possibility with a PA and my manual chair. It is far too big a risk to let luggage handlers deal with my powerchair, so I would always travel abroad with my manual. I say 'would' because I now have my manual / power chair. This is fantastic at airports because it can be used as a powerchair right up until you get to the boarding gate then you simply take the battery out and put it in your hand luggage and it becomes a manual to the baggage handlers. Unless I stay somewhere familiar, my thoughts are always with the bathroom where I will be staying. Whilst still able to transfer and wash myself I need to ensure that this will still be possible wherever I am staying. Hand rails need to be in the right place, a roll in shower needs to be there and there must be access for my legs under the sink. If the bathroom has these 3 things then I am happy to go. Trying to find this out though is not so easy. An 'accessible bathroom' listed in brochures or websites may not be 'accessible' for me. This is something I have learned with experience. For instance a bedroom with an 'en suite and fully accessible bathroom interior' is of no use to me if there is not enough space between the wall and the bed for me in my chair to reach the bathroom to get into it. People so often do not join up the dots in terms of access.

Access is of course not just about the physical environment. For instance, some countries are more accommodating than others with language differences and this is so often an issue for both able and disabled English people. In some countries, people will accept that you can only speak English and accommodate that as best they can. Others will only accept their own language and will not help you out. We English are generally quite lazy when it comes to language. Our attitude is: We'll wait for you to speak English, not learn your language. Also in terms of 'attitudes' to disability, most European countries are pretty similar in my experience. Attitudes and language can be as big a barrier to access as steps and narrow doorways.

Having discussed cars and planes, there is currently just one other viable mode of transport for me and that is trains. I recently took a trip to Switzerland, taking the Eurostar to Paris, a taxi across Paris and then a train to Basel. This was an amazingly smooth journey. Wheelchair facilities on trains are by and large very good now. They have improved a great deal over the last 10/20 years, in the UK especially. I think improvements to stations could still be made though (ramps are needed to board all trains in the UK). This could be easily overcome by increasing the height of platforms or even by having automatic ramps drop down from the foot of every train door when the train stops at each station. Access to platforms at many stations could also be improved. It is impossible for me to travel in both directions from my nearest train station as I can't cross the railway line because there is an inaccessible bridge.

I flew on my own on a short flight to Newcastle from London. It was the one and only flight I made alone. It was back in 1995, just a few years after my diagnosis of ataxia. I was a wheelchair user but could walk down the aisle of an aeroplane supporting myself on the seats as I walked (stumbled). Not long into the flight, food and drink was served. I ate my food and poured myself a glass of water. I took a sip and put the plastic glass down on the 'pull down' table in front of me. Swallowing liquids can often make me cough and if I still have hold of the cup at this time it is very likely that anyone within close proximity would be in danger of becoming rather wet as I would throw my drink all over them whilst trying not to drop my cup. I then swallowed the sip of water, coughed and then the involuntary movement of my legs meant that my knees hit the table hovering just above them and the cup and contents went straight over the seat in front of me and landed on its' incumbent . My fellow passenger turned round and stared at me with outrage and dismay. All I could do was look embarrassed and say sorry.

My travels have included almost every continent on the globe. Europe of course has seen me visiting the most countries of any continent, sixteen in all, as it is the one that the UK sits inside. It is true to say that most of my visits there have involved away football fixtures coupled with occasional day trips to places of interest, most of which are the ones like Pompeii and Mount Vesuvius which most attracted me as a boy when learning about volcanoes at school. I have visited Asia, Australasia [Pics 19 & 25], Africa [Pic 5] and the United States and Canada too, often with just a PA and sometimes as part of a larger group of disabled people and their carers/ PA's. As you can see my own travels have been extensive with South America being the only continent I have not visited, although if you include Antarctica as a continent, as you should, I have not been there either. Without question I would love to visit Brazil as I studied this country and the Amazon River when I was a small boy and this would make it an ideal trip. Maybe one day I will get a chance to be there especially for me and my interests, as the next two biggest shows on Earth are there, the 2014 Football World Cup and the 2016 Olympics.

One trip which merits particular mention is my trip to Hong Kong in 1994 because it came only a year after my becoming a wheelchair user and was my first trip outside of Europe. This trip was a mammoth one, organised as it was by Surrey PHAB (Physically Handicapped, Able Bodied as was, the terminology has since changed thank goodness) for 40 people, few of whom knew each other before. It had been clearly stated before we left that the accommodation and facilities were of a basic nature, so I didn't expect much as I headed to my room. I was not disappointed! I was in Room 2 which was the first room on the right in the accommodation block. I was sharing a room with 3 others - Graham, Andy and Martin. As I was the first to reach the room I had first option on beds so I made my choice and headed off to check out the bathroom facilities. They were basic too but it is worthwhile mentioning here as I have talked about before, that when one uses a wheelchair it is better to have accessible, basic amenities than lavish, posh ones that you can't get to or use. Yes, it was all very basic but it suited my needs perfectly. The holiday was filled with excursions and events and was quite tiring for us all particularly our stoic helpers.

Fairly early on in the holiday we went to the Central District of Hong Kong for a guided tour of the Governor's House. We arrived a bit late (the bus driver having slight navigational problems i.e. - didn't know where the hell it was). We were made very welcome none the less and were given a very accurate, detailed speech about the history of the house. We were allowed to see all of the downstairs - the lounge, dining room, hall etc. and a group photo was taken in the ballroom. I was both surprised and pleased to see that there was more than adequate wheelchair access both inside the house and in its ample surrounding area. See! It is possible! I was honestly and reliably informed that the ramps outside were installed more for baggage and waste transportation than for disabled people, but they certainly served us well. This trip had been advertised as a holiday of a lifetime and I could not disagree.

In conclusion, other than driving my own car, and before using a wheelchair and accessible vehicle, travel had always been something that my disability had limited. I used to think: How could I keep safe whilst driving? How could I cope at an airport with all that walking? When would I be able to mount a train going in either direction at my local station? I have greatly appreciated and continue to do so, the means to travel in a wheelchair since my ataxia has progressed and will no doubt advance further in the future, it now being impossible to physically put one foot in front of the other without falling over. However, being a wheelchair user has made it even more possible to travel than ever it was before. It has always filled me with excitement to make a minimum amount of effort for example transferring out of my wheelchair to another seat, and to arrive in a totally different place after an amount of time. I enjoy travelling away due to experiencing different cultures, attitudes and ways of living and I enjoy the journey home because I always look forward to my home comforts and routine. I feel that my ability to travel will remain exactly the same. The major change for me will be the psychological adjustments I must make to accept more help (personal assistance and care) whilst keeping my mind focussed on enjoying my travels. As disability becomes accepted and access needs are recognised, these major changes need to be balanced by a more disabled friendly world and improved attitudes towards disabled people.

I am coming around slowly to the idea of travel on water. The first time I had been on a boat using a wheelchair happened just before my ataxia diagnosis and that trip was a success, it being quite easy to get on and off the boat. They have never figured high in my list of priorities but as my ataxia progresses they seem to be a good option for a holiday. I am considering a Caribbean cruise and as everyone knows there are many more options for travelling to far flung places on these floating entertainment palaces. Of course they are expensive holidays and as I need a PA at all times costs can mount up but for those holidays of a lifetime taking in many different locations in a short space of time they are a good option.

Chapter 5.
My PAs.

Direct Payments is a government initiative administered by social services. This gives users money directly to fund their own care rather than them having to rely on the traditional route of a local government authority giving them their own care. It came into force in 1997 and I was one of the first people to use it in 1998. I was still working at this time and the care I required was minimal. I used to employ just two people for three hours each per week. One to clean my house from top to bottom (the very same cleaner, Doreen has only just left my employment after more than nineteen years.) and one who met me at Sainsbury's to help me do my weekly food shop; Liz. The role of a Personal Assistant (PA) will vary with each disabled person and with the life they lead. A PA is just that; someone to assist a disabled person in doing anything they need or want to do. This need or want must be an assessed one by social services.

My ataxia means I need help to carry out many of my daily activities but I have never found it easy to ask anyone for help. As ataxia is a progressive disease I have not always had care needs, unlike now. Looking back, the care needs I had in my earlier life (from say, the age of 15) amounted to making food and drinks and these needs were all met by my parents and latterly by my work colleagues. Back in the early days of my using a wheelchair (aged 24-30) I enjoyed caring for myself, my daily tasks would use up the majority of the day outside of work but I became accustomed to this and knew no different. However, when I began to need PAs as my condition worsened, I was fortunate indeed that the 'Direct Payments' scheme had come into force.

When I drew up an advert for my first proper PA, the fact that I couldn't manage alone anymore was mortifying to me and extremely painful, but the necessity for one could not be put off any longer. I tried to think how this situation differed from the support I got from family and my work colleagues, mentioned above. I realised that the latter support was in part unconditional in the case of my family, as that's what families do for each other. Probably in the case of my workplace, and in the context of disability discrimination, two things may have been at play: a legal requirement and also a case of human nature where people do help out when they are in close proximity to a person in need. In a sense I didn't need to ask for this kind of support; it was simply there by default. Now for the first time I was forced to admit that, in order to achieve real independence, that I needed support. This meant asking for help and this did not sit well with me, although I relished the management of my future care needs as discussed later in this chapter. To this day I still get similar feelings of humiliation and mortification, although over time I guess these feelings have subsided somewhat. This is an ongoing process though and I face these challenges each time my care needs change.

I still use the same template now to advertise for a domestic help PA although obviously I have added to it and amended it over the years. By 'domestic help PA' I mean someone who assists me with my daily activities around the house such as receiving and putting away the shopping delivery, making my bed, cooking, helping me stand in my frame and ride my cycle etc. My other PAs are more friends than PAs. They are just people I go out to places with or go on holiday with. Some of these PAs were friends that sort of became 'PAs' or 'domestic help PAs who have become friends. Having said that, the roles and hence responsibilities for the majority of my PAs (I have a team of 9 at the moment) have evolved over time as my disability has progressed. My interests and needs are pretty much the same but it would be fair to say that my PAs have to work a little harder now than before.

At first I was apprehensive and felt a bit daunted by the thought of being an employer, but I have realised that an interview is nothing more, as the employer anyway, than an informal chat. This is a chance to see how I think I might get on with a prospective PA: to check whether we connect or not. I know exactly what duties they will have to perform, and they are clear in advance about them also through my advert and information pack. Their application apprises me of their skills and experience, so I can focus on our bond what I would call the 'softer' side of things. As it stands all my hiring and firing has been done verbally. None of my PAs have asked me for a contract and I am quite happy not to give them one as with an informal arrangement, employment laws are all irrelevant. Long may I never have to issue a contract! As long as everything is well documented and both parties agree then I see no problem.

I must say I thoroughly enjoy the written and organisational part of being an employer. I am used to, and indeed enjoy, calculating and recording the wages and I like using online banking to pay all my staff. I also take pleasure in writing letters (on Microsoft Word) and I record all details using Microsoft Excel Spreadsheet. I became confident in using this in my working life for the MOD. I used to manage a £140 million defence budget on an Excel spreadsheet so managing £4,000 a quarter is relatively simple for me. Employment law says that I am obliged to do all of this but it is not a chore.

As my life stands now, I could not function as a person without PAs. My life would be nothing without them. They have become vitally important to me. Without them my quality of life would plummet and I'm pretty sure my state of well-being would soon follow. Listing the benefits would be an exhaustive task, but they fall into two major categories. Firstly the practical, those tasks which are if not impossible, in some cases, then at least extremely difficult and time consuming and secondly the more important, in my view, the emotional. My PAs are a lifeline and a connection to the outside world. This is why it is so important in an interview to find out how much empathy a prospective PA has with me and with my situation. It is good to have people to talk to on a basic level and to share important parts of my life with. Therefore I need a friendly, respectful and reliable person. The best way to make this point is to point to a couple of people I have had trouble with once they have become my PAs:

1. One woman proved unreliable as she would text me the night before the morning she was due to come round and say she couldn't make it. This went on for the first two weeks of her employ so I let her go in a similar way - by text message! I had not employed her for this, but to be a responsible

worker, someone who turns up when they say they are going to, is paramount.

2. Another woman was a bit different; she was reliable, trustworthy, and honest and a good time keeper but I never felt comfortable in her company. She spoke perfect English as she'd been in this country for seven years and had married an Englishman. However, she made me feel like her boss. I know this sounds strange because that is exactly what I am, but I've never felt like a boss with any other of my PAs and when I'm in my own home I don't particularly want to feel like that. She would stand about waiting for my instructions all the time. I employed her for three months, waiting for her to settle in and become more relaxed and hoping for our relationship to become friendlier but it didn't. Every day it was 'employee' and 'client'. I became very unhappy at the situation and had to do something. As she had been an employee for 3 months I thought I owed her an explanation so I phoned her. I thought back to how I'd been sacked 26 years ago. "Grace" I said nervously. "It's Matthew. I'm sorry but I'm going to have to let you go" I then did my best to explain why. I followed this up with a letter too and she seemed to accept it ok. I had also been deducting tax from her wages but found out from my payroll services company that she didn't have to pay tax so I could repay all this to her in one go. Perhaps she saw this as a parting present! See! I am a good and fair man and not an overbearing boss!

So to clarify I need the following in a 'good PA': An ability to get on with them, (are they good company?); reliability hence dependability; honesty (can you trust them?); good timekeeping and of course an ability to do the job. As my PAs are working in my home it really is crucial to get on well. I am very house proud, I have a place for everything with everything in its place. I do not like anyone in my house that I do not like. It is vitally important that I feel comfortable with a PA whilst they are working alongside me. I am able to judge a good PA by whether or not I want them in my home. If I get on well with someone, I enjoy having them around.

To be a little more specific about the duties of a PA and without boring the reader, as things stand during the day I need to cycle my medi-motion machine. I also stand for half an hour and eat a meal. My PA will help with all that (cooking meals and maybe cutting up the food) and help with things like putting the shopping away, taking me to appointments, washing up, cleaning the house, loading / unloading the washing machine. Basically all the things I need to do but can't do myself. I can and do wash up when my PAs are not working.

I also need assistance in accessing the community: My PA will just be my driver and my ears really. When it comes to trying to hear with a lot of background noise, my hearing is very poor.

A specific activity which I am still undertaking was first suggested to me by my PA Jess in the early summer of 2011, this is Carriage Driving with the local Riding for the Disabled Association (RDA) at Merrist Wood. Merrist Wood is a 400 acre outdoor College offering academic courses in land-based subjects specialising in equine and animal care. On Wednesday mornings a group of around 30 horse owners, qualified carriage drivers, volunteers and people with ranging disabilities and their PAs gather together to enable 3 or 4 carriages to be driven around the site, through woods and across the countryside by the disabled members.

I remain in my wheelchair to drive and am pushed onto the carriage using 2 ramps. Each disabled person is accompanied by an able bodied driver for health and safety reasons and so there are two people with one set of reigns each on each carriage. We all gather together each Christmas for a meal and awards are given out at the end of the afternoon. At the end of the first year I received the 'Best Newcomer' award and on a very wet day in May 2012 I entered my first competition [Pic 3] and came 4th in the Royal Windsor Horseshow (RDA Section) and was awarded my rosette by none other than the Duke of Edinburgh. You can see me shaking his hand elsewhere in this book. (Pic 4)

I still am accompanied there by a PA (now Miriam) every Wednesday and I really enjoy the freedom I get in being able to control the horse and I also enjoy the views we get out in the countryside and the feel of the air rushing by my cheeks.

Going further afield i.e. abroad, is when my PA is much more needed. I am paying a PA to be with me all day, every day and this is because I am out of my natural environment. As I am also on holiday I want to spend my energy having fun rather than getting myself clothed, which I normally do at home, but which I get a PA to help me with on holiday. They will assist me far more with daily tasks and pushing me in my wheelchair as it is not always possible to take my manual / power chair. My PAs also need to drive the car around when I am abroad.

As I mentioned earlier none of my PAs have been on employment contracts. The drawback to this informality is that a PA has to give no notice that they will leave, but I do feel this arrangement makes for a more informal working relationship which is the way I like it. I still have all my employer responsibilities to fulfil like leave entitlement, hours of work, sick leave, holiday leave & pay etc. When someone leaves suddenly I then find that I am a bit rushed to find a replacement and as finding the right PA is a difficult task anyway this can cause some anxiety and stress. As I have said before I have found that if you get on well with PAs and can relate to them then it is easy to keep them happy in their work.

No matter how often you think to yourself 'They're only with me because I pay them', it still hits you hard when a PA leaves your employment. A PA is paid to look after your welfare. If I get on well with a PA then it follows that that person becomes a friend of mine. No matter how hard you try and tell yourself that to them, you are just a job, a means for them to earn money, you can't help but become attached to someone who is looking after your welfare. When this bond has been formed it is very difficult to break. Not all PAs choose to stay in touch when they have left either. So not only have you lost a PA but you have lost a friend. It can feel like a bit of a betrayal but I try to think of it from their perspective too. Often people may move away or have commitments in new jobs or with family which limit their time and availability. It can be a very unsettling time though trying to find a new PA whilst mourning the loss of an old one. I guess the best sort of PA is one that you don't regard as a friend but one who you don't mind being in your house! If only it were that easy.

I cannot live my current or future life without my PAs. They are my lifeblood, the oil that makes the engine of my life work. They help me to fulfil almost every aspect of my life from the daily tasks to my emotional life. Their assistance allows me to live in many ways a fuller life than I led before I had my diagnosis and I expect as I age and as my condition worsens I shall rely on them even more.

Chapter 6.
My Special Home.

Looking back to the first time I moved out of the parental home, the first thing I did once I had set my computer up in the new place, was to write a letter to my parents, thanking them for bringing me up and for looking after me but that now I needed to take charge of my own life and I needed to feel like a person myself rather than their disabled son. One of the positives that has come out of living my own life for 20 years is that every day I am making them proud of me for living alone and providing for myself.

What does it mean to me to live alone? I had always had a need for self-reliance. When I was with mum and dad I have to admit that independence was difficult. Now, I love my autonomy and being able to do what I want, when I want to do it. I definitely had a massive sense of achievement only a couple of weeks after I moved out of my parent's house and then had started to work through the access issues I encountered at my own place, but now standing on my own two feet is simply normal for me.

My dad took my leaving home very badly initially. When I first said to him I had contacted the council about moving out, my dad went white as a sheet. He no doubt thought I stood no chance of being able to live alone and he was worried for me. Surrey Heath Housing Association offered me the house after I had written to Surrey Heath Borough Council. I had met a housing officer at my parents' house shortly after and I was able to tell her what I needed and why my parent's house was not right for me. My parents both knew I needed to be independent and also that their house was not suitable anymore, so over time this may have made it easier for them to let go. The anxious bit for me, in the early stages, was the ten months between my finding out I had ataxia and when I moved out and into my new home on 25th October, 1993. During this time I had worked out exactly what I needed but it was as yet out of reach which was very frustrating. It was a lot more difficult for me than an able-bodied person. Of course, if anyone is going to move it is unsettling, but I was waiting to move and also to become my 'own person', to be able to do things myself, waiting to make myself a cup of tea.

I was in my house within seven months after making the first contact with the council. It seemed it was all done on a points basis and when you are disabled you get more points. Because I had had no experience of living in a wheelchair before, my first home in Chobham was, in retrospect, far from ideal. It was a little small but I thought I would have it anyway, as I was desperate to move out of home and I was sure I could make it work. As I had up to that time lived only in the family home with the support of my parents, I had no idea of what to look for in my own place. It was only by using a trial and error process that I developed this home. The place was a ground floor flat, all on one level, with its front door around the side, as it had been converted from a single house. In effect my front door was the house's back door. It had a square hallway with three doors, one to the bathroom, one to the bedroom and one to the lounge leading to the kitchen. The kitchen was big enough for a fridge and a washing machine but the freezer had to go in the hallway. There was also a sink but not much cupboard space at all. But, I was in my first house and I felt free, empowered and in control of my life for the first time. Independence was so vital to me and enabled me to do everything for myself for the first time. I took on the most mundane of tasks previously covered by my parents and this felt scary but more than anything, exciting.

In 1993, although using a wheelchair for most mobility requirements, I could still stand up by hanging onto rails which were soon conveniently placed where I needed them, thanks to dad. The bathroom only had a bath which was not too much of a problem as I could still get out of a wheelchair and into a bath but eventually I asked the council to install a shower. In this case as with many other improvements I have made I have never relied on Occupational Therapists, as mine have always been rubbish, not doing much, except offering advice that was not useful and taking too long and working within financial constraints. I asked for assistance once when I felt my toilet seat was too high. Thinking about money, they offered a leg lifting device. Not good! So I have always found it better to organise things myself.

After 7 years in Chobham the internet came out and I was doing a lot of surfing and becoming increasingly frustrated that my area did not have broadband access yet. I knew however that Bagshot did have it. This helped me to decide that I needed to get over to a new home nearer my parents. My first home had been a place for me to work out everything I was likely to need in the future and I am grateful to have had the opportunity. Another major issue for me had been that it did not have two means of access, which in the case of fire was very dangerous for me. Health & Safety had become a big issue at this time and so could be used to help lever me out of Chobham.

I had to find a way, another reason why my Chobham home was unsuitable so I told the council that my kitchen was too small, which it was. This meant it was possible to get a new flat as my needs were not being met at the existing place. I had done as much as was possible to get the Chobham house adapted including getting an architect to design an extension in which to host a new kitchen. However, after all my efforts it was decided that it would be more cost effective to re-house me. I was in regular contact with them outlining my needs and when they first showed me a new place, my current home, I said to them I would need to have the place significantly modified in order to move in. The major consideration in moving for me was the access to broadband, not that I told them this, so I also asked what the telephone number of the new house was to check for its availability there before I said yes. Once I had these two assurances I agreed to the house and then the work could begin. The previous house had been a good learning experience and taught me things and I also knew better what I was entitled to. I had no real issues because I knew exactly what I wanted and knew who to approach.

'I was once woken up to the sound of my cat 'meowing' with something in her mouth. This is a familiar sound I would imagine to all cat owners. Zola (for 'tis her name) had brought this (later discovered to be a mouse) in through the cat-flap and was now in my bedroom. She then released the mouse from her mouth and began chasing it around my bedroom. In scurrying round the bedroom she knocked my coat off it's' hanger which I leave on the door handle of my wardrobe. After ten minutes or so Zola lost

the mouse and was just watching and waiting for it to re-appear. I decided to get up as I was well awake by then anyway so I transferred to my wheelchair. To return the bedroom to some normality I leant down from my wheelchair to pick up my coat from the floor and the mouse shot out from underneath it. It made me jump alarmingly (Startled reaction) and I fell out my wheelchair and hit my head on the plasterboard wall. You can still see the indent on the wall to this day. Fortunately I did no serious damage to myself. I was not wearing my seatbelt as I was thinking only of my coat on the floor as soon as I got in my chair. I had to call the paramedics of course to pick me up off the floor and they checked me out as I told them I'd hit my head.

So the major and crucial point I had in mind both in having a bigger house and as a wheelchair user, was to design my new home in such a way as to leave as much space in the main part of each room as possible. This was to maximise my ability to move around without obstruction; something all wheelchair users are extremely conscious of. With this in mind and now describing my new home in sequence, firstly, I needed much more room in the kitchen. In the beginning the back door was there, taking up valuable wall space, so I got them to move it to my bedroom. This meant that in the kitchen I could fit in all my white goods and more work surfaces and a hob and a sink at the right level. Then I had a breakfast bar fitted which enabled me to get food out of the microwave and slide it across without a problem. I also got a fridge freezer with the fridge on top and freezer below. In my previous place the work surfaces were already there so it was more difficult to effect change. In the new place I knew I wanted and needed lower surfaces and on 3 different levels. The fitter was surprised, he thought I was mad, but as I explained one had to be the perfect height for my knees, one had to be the same plus 3 inches to allow for a shallow sink and the other needed to be another 3 inches higher with the washing machine underneath it. So the fitter's disbelief aside, I knew what I wanted and was not prepared to be dictated to about it and he did the work to my requirements. The Occupational Therapist who I guess was there to advise me on what I needed just watched with interest.

I was once eating breakfast, sneezed, and fell out my wheelchair. After that I have always worn a seatbelt whilst in my wheelchair. This incident helped to shape my view on how to keep safe whilst in my wheelchair in the future, and shaped my ideas in the new house.

In the bathroom I also asked for a roll-in shower because it had had a bath at first, and I needed a toilet with a floor-to-ceiling pole as a rail could not be placed on the wall adjacent to it because the wall ended and the doorway started. However this did reduce the space available to enter the room in my wheelchair. This was not a problem until I got my manual / power chair because this chair is about 3 inches wider than my manual chair. Because of this I had the pole taken down and a rail put on the frame of the door. This is an example of some of the minor changes that are needed to keep things running smoothly for me in my home. I also needed a sink that I could get my legs under and a wheel-in shower with a drop-down shower chair.

I purchased three further floor-to-ceiling poles, one in the lounge next to my automatic reclining 2-piece sofa, and two in the bedroom, one next to my bed and one by the space at the bottom of my bed where I left my powerchair when I wasn't using it. I have since removed this pole as I no longer need to transfer between manual and powerchair. These 'floor-to-ceiling' poles are very effective in my being able to transfer from my wheelchair to toilet / bed / sofa by pulling myself up, twisting round and then dropping down. I now have a rubber mat at the base of each as otherwise transferring with naked feet meant I would often slip.

After some time I had a front door fitted, a big job paid for by me, as I got frustrated with the time it was taking social services. The door is operated by remote control. This is good to be able to see a car pull up outside whilst sitting behind my desk and to be able to open the door for people without delay and without having to move. Before this, when the doorbell rang I would be under immediate pressure to get to the door, something that my body does not respond well to. Also worth mentioning here is the net bag I have attached to the back of the front door behind the letter box. This catches all my daily post so I don't have to spend time picking it all up from the floor.

Other adaptations which have proved most useful for me are: window winders (of which more later) which help me to be able to open and close my windows; long pulleys for the curtains and the blinds; a specialist bed that raises up at the back for sitting and raises underneath my legs so I can be comfortable when lying down asleep; an electrically operated recliner sofa, as I mentioned a minute ago, this actually is not a 'designed for the disabled' sofa but a standard one purchased from DFS; and my standing frame a crucial piece of equipment in maintaining my ability to stand, stretching my calf muscles and in improving my blood circulation.

Apart from the kitchen fitter, most people have trusted the things I want, so the only issue I have faced is the cost of things. I was and am fortunate to be in a reasonable financial position so I have always felt that I would much rather get the things I need 'now' and pay for them, rather than rely on Social Services. I did get a wall knocked down and a wall bricked up, expensive at £36,000, (this amount also included all the fittings in the kitchen and bathroom, flooring for both as well as levelling the access in and out of the bungalow at the back and front but I used a grant from an external body and this was achieved on my behalf by the Housing Association. The council did all this work for, and in consultation with, me. The builders also did the decoration and my dad made the finishing touches and I paid for professionals to do other things, like installing window winders, blinds and carpets. Other than this I have had an awning put up at the back, by a PA of mine at the time, a patio and some decking also in the back garden, but I also managed to convince the council to dig deep into its coffers to pay to provide a path and a shed for me to house my scooter. I have long since sold the scooter using first my powerchair and now my manual / power chair instead.

This second house felt very different to the first one. The independence I had achieved before this move was built upon, and the fact that the house was far superior and I was far more confident in my needs had a lot to do with this very different feel. I brought all my experience from the first house into this new place. I had hardly used a wheelchair at all when I moved to my first home but now I had learnt about the space I needed and I brought this experience to bear in the new place. I am still very happy here and sort out problems as they arise always in isolation which seems less stressful. For example, I recently bought a new combination manual and power wheelchair, mentioned earlier, a great and positive development for me, of which more later, but one which has caused another problem. I previously had a carpet in the house but the chair in manual mode was very heavy to handle, it having two motors built in to the wheels, so now my solution has been to have a vinyl tiling flooring throughout which makes life much easier. I always learn by experience!

I have no real desire to have new adaptations, but if I did, I am sure I would work them out. My past experience is crucial in making sure that things will proceed to be sorted as and when they arise. I suppose the thought of further adaptations is difficult for me as it would indicate a worsening of my condition. However, one thing which I am looking into for the future is a patient turner which I have in my house in Spain. In my home in the UK I cannot get off the sofa unless someone else is there to hold the turner. The only way for me in five years would be to have a patient turner fixed to the floor, with one by the toilet and one by the bed. This would mean I would not need to have someone else with me. It works by planting your feet on either side of the top plate, and your PA can turn you around easily, which means you don't have to use your body and feet to get rotated. I suppose the dreaded hoist may be needed, eventually, if I lose the use of my body, but I would rather not think about that right now. I used one once on a trip away when I fell out of bed and the friends PA came with a mobile hoist. It felt very undignified. Darren who lives down the road uses a hoist as his Muscular Dystrophy prevents him using his arms to pull himself upright. He is never on his own, he is always with a PA or his girlfriend and this makes it difficult to talk to him about the use of his hoist and get his true feelings. He always seems absolutely fine, but I am sure he must have down days with it all.

Back to one of the recurring and simplest tasks that has engaged me throughout my life, *tea making*! As I have said before this domestic chore has always been from the beginning of my illness, one that was most likely to give my growing physical problems away. In the beginning my parents assisted me by always making drinks for me, something which is not so unusual, but later once I moved out of the parental home it became clear I needed to sort this task out once and for all to avoid potentially dangerous accidents. As I have said I for many years have been using a tipping device which my kettle sits in thus avoiding the necessity to lift the kettle up off its stand and pour the water into the cup using arm strength and coordination. An alternative is an electric hot water boiler from Breville called 'One Cup' or 'Hot Cup'. This is a hot water dispenser that boils and releases the water directly to a single mug or cup placed beneath it. They are quite expensive but have a couple of great benefits, namely they facilitate the safe and effective delivery of a single cup of boiled water and also in so doing save energy and therefore costs.

Of course pouring the boiling water is not the only challenge in successfully making hot drinks. There is often a need to transport it to a more comfortable part of the home in order to drink it. As a wheelchair user I find a 'bean-bag' lap tray is best as sits comfortably on my knees providing an ideal flat surface on which to carry things. If I were to cough or sneeze as I was carrying my drink on a tray like this, it may take me a good hour to mop the drink off the floor! Generally though 'bean-bag' lap trays have always and will continue to play an important role in maintaining my independence within my home.

Although I was using a wheelchair full time when I moved into my current home nearly twelve years ago, it was becoming increasingly unsafe for me to pull myself up out of the chair to reach window handles to open the windows. Therefore, to make things easier for me I arranged for my house to be fitted with window winders. These are winding handles placed close to windows that push a thick chain within a tube to a window opening in order to open and close the window. It means you can control the opening and closing of windows without struggling out of your chair. I have every opening window in my home fitted with winder controls (8 in total). They are expensive (mine were a total of £900) but it was useful for me to have them fitted after my furniture was in place. They are now probably a standard fitting in a new disabled friendly home.

Technology plays its part but I certainly cannot envisage needing more anytime soon. I have pulleys and remotes already and it is always possible to get things done by pressing a button. I think though that sometimes things like these make us lazy. You have to go on doing things as long as you possibly can. It is cheating yourself if you have things put in place to make things easier for you when you don't need it. I did find it was becoming a chore several years ago to circle my house turning off all the lights before going to bed. I found out about these remote sockets which are all operated by remote control. I put one of them on the socket to each light in my house and also each of my TV's. I can now not leave the TV's in 'standby' mode and turn off all my lights in five seconds rather than five minutes. So there are times where technology can save time or make life easier but in general my philosophy is 'I will struggle on until such time as it becomes impossible for me.'

I love my home and envisage staying here forever. The only time I would have to move is if I wanted to live with a fellow wheelchair user. It does cause difficulties now when friends using wheelchairs visit but I am living an independent life at the moment so I do not ever see me having to move. My original Occupational Therapist from the time when I moved in told me that because it is a bungalow and has strong roof joists when and if eventually I need a motorised rail fitted, it could be sorted with not too much effort.

I decided last year that I would begin to start making my front and back gardens look more pleasing on the eye. I wanted a more colourful and attractive look. I have a hose and a sprinkler system in my back garden and I had a hose fitted out the front last year so I now have the ability to keep both front and back gardens watered. None of my current team of PA's have the knowledge of flowers so I now employ a gardener (Gill) who has given me two gardens to be really proud of.

I rate my home ten out of ten for accessibility. There is not a thing I need or want to improve right now. When I was having problems with getting in and out of my car I could not find a solution until my disabled neighbour mentioned the vehicle I now have, so new ideas are always welcome. I think it is important to try and stay abreast of new technologies and gadgets.

Chapter 7.

Two Diagnoses.

Despite the changes in my physical abilities that I had been experiencing since the age of 12-13 these only crystallised in my mind upon receiving my first diagnosis of Charcot-Marie Tooth disease (CMT) when I was 18 years old. When I was given this conclusion to my growing disability I felt nothing, I simply couldn't associate myself with it. I remember thinking 'I can't have a disease, I don't feel sick - I'm fine.' All I could think of was getting out of the hospital and focussing on something that I found enjoyable in my life, instead of being in a place with all these people with limps and medical problems.

Strictly speaking I have in my life received three diagnoses in all, quite enough for anyone to handle. The very first diagnosis was of Osgood-Schlatter disease, a condition which is curable with the use of supports and gentle exercise of the muscles around the knees. It only takes a physical exam too, so I didn't need to have complex tests or anything like that. This diagnosis was not in place for long though as my condition was markedly worsening, not that I admitted it even to myself.

I had a number of further tests once it became obvious that my condition was not Osgood-Schlatter disease. The second diagnosis of Charcot-Marie-Tooth disease (CMT) was kept from me at first or so I remember but, it is more likely that having been told I refused to hear it. Having been told that what I had was curable, it was a terrible shock to be told that I had something else. I actually imagined at the time that the diagnosis was given to my parents instead, a fact which in itself led to more than a few problems over the years. With this more serious diagnosis of CMT I buried my head in the sand and just got on with life. I avoided discussing it at all with my parents. Shortly after the diagnosis I began writing a diary and telling it my secret thoughts and disappointments, all of the angsts of my teenage life, which seemed to be compounded by my awkward walking and resulting instability. This was the most difficult period in my life, much more difficult than the subsequent years spent dealing with my ataxia and the adaptations I needed to make my life the positive experience it is today.

When I look back at events in my life at this time I remember I was very nervous as I sat in the waiting room at Farnham Road Hospital, Guildford in early 1987. My parents and I had arrived 15 minutes early for our appointment, as we always did (and indeed still do) and these minutes were amongst some of the most nerve wracking I've ever experienced. I was scared to find out why being aged 12 or 13 I had noticed the following which had left me confused and scared:

- I had my football ability seriously decrease
- I had gone from group A in games at school in the second year to group D in the 5th year
- I had been forced to give up cricket at the age of 15 (after having struggled for a year or two)
- I had seen my ability to play table tennis drastically reduced
- I had become unable to carry drinks full to the brim without spilling them
- I had become ever more uncomfortable when walking.

So here I was, anxious as hell, sitting with my parents who wanted answers, even to get some kind of diagnosis. I can't begin to tell you how I felt when Dr Patten told me the disease he thought I had, at the time I could not remember exactly what it was called, and as I couldn't read the Doctor's writing my ignorance was blissfully complete. I was also told that I had to go to the hospital for 36 hours on Thursday and Friday of that same week. I was to spend my first ever night in a hospital bed. Then I was asked if I would attend a doctor's training seminar on the Saturday so they could try and work out what is wrong with me. In other words try me out as a guinea pig. Apparently, I was one of only 20,000 people with this disease in Britain.

My whole life flashed past me on the way back from Guildford. All the great sporting moments of my so far short life including my entire Curley Park Rangers boys football career [Pics 22, 23 & 26] with 99 goals, my school football career, the Connaught 4 - a - side football tournaments, all the sprint races I had won (even for the district), my Bagshot Cricket Club and Frimley Table Tennis Club appearances and my solitary district football appearance, loomed large in my mind. I had won boy of the week at Butlins for table tennis seven years previously. I showed such potential and promise at sport, I was good at all of them. At school I was amongst the best at most of them. Now deep down I suppose I knew I could never be that good again.

Thursday soon came around and I was grateful that I had not had to wait for too long before this stay in hospital. During my stay several doctors saw me, and asked the same old questions and did the same old tests - testing reflexes and such. During my stay specimens were taken including blood, I had a heart examination (ECG) and also finally an E.E.G. where wires and rods were attached to my head to monitor my eye to brain and ear to brain reaction times. This all took 90 minutes so why I had to be in hospital for two days is beyond me. I tried not to think of it too much and put on a brave face for those people who knew, my family of course. Those who didn't know me well saw nothing different in me, or at least that's how I saw it. I had been told I would know of my diagnosis for sure by Saturday.

After Saturday's Doctor's training seminar my diagnosis was confirmed. When you are told by a doctor that it is impossible to maintain the level of sporting prowess that you are used to, it kind of hits you. I was not the only one either. Dad cried when he was discussing it with mum back at home later. I had never seen him cry before and it upset me. As for me I cried as soon as I got back too. I don't know how I held back the tears that long even. At that moment, nothing else seemed to matter: A-Levels; a job; even snooker didn't matter, which was for me desperate indeed. I needed time to sort myself out, time to adjust my mind. I had decisions to make like who to tell for a start. I had decided that it was best to tell no one, at least not until it was 100% certain. I was still hoping that the new tests I had been scheduled to have would tell me I was alright, that this was something I would grow out of. Now I knew, although one good thing that was said that day was that my condition should not get any worse. I thought at least that if that were true I would be OK. However, when you are told there is no cure it still hurts a lot.

Later in 1987 I was sent for physiotherapy at our local hospital, Frimley Park, and on the first visit dad even had to explain to the physiotherapist how this condition had come about, which is more than I knew or even wanted to know. It didn't come about in my book; it was just the way I was. Thankfully they agreed to explain things to Dr Lee from what we had told them and what they could see in me when I had been doing the exercises they prescribed.

Following this stint of physiotherapy and as time went on, my legs were feeling more and more as though they had lead weights in them and my eyesight was becoming blurred. I had pains in the muscles of my left arm too. I had days which were terribly bad, with my legs stiff as boards and with awful balance. This was when I was most likely to fall especially down stairs or steps. I had had trouble with one of my cars too because it had a stiff clutch and made my legs ache. I began to take notice of various TV programs about disability. One was about a man with motor neurone disease, but Dad said that that was nothing to do with me, although it was something I was not convinced about because no one seemed to know much about my condition anyway. I thought Dr Patten had mentioned motor neurone disease before, so I was racked with worry for a time. He had also said though that I would lead a normal life as the disease was fully developed but I thought, no I *knew*, it was getting worse. Another programme was focussed on Glyn Worsnip, a well-known radio and TV broadcaster best known for his appearances on 'That's Life' who had an incurable brain disease. All of these things coupled with what I knew was a progressively worsening physical condition were worrying me a lot.

After a short while I made a decision to go to see Dr Patten alone at the Royal Surrey Hospital in Guildford and get all the information on this CMT thing I had been told I had. I was nervous about telling my parents about this, but I knew I had to know for myself. Eventually I got round to telling them and of course they understood why I wanted to go alone. Mum gave me a list of questions for him, so I could ask him more about my condition. I was in a strange position; I needed to know exactly what was wrong with me but in a way I preferred not to know as it depressed me and I would rather have thought about happier things. Mum was right though, it was my future at stake and I needed to know all the consequences and realities of my condition. One question on mum's list was about whether my condition might carry a disability allowance, although I would have to be registered disabled, which I didn't like the sound of.

I subsequently applied for Disability Living Allowance and got it at the lower rate. I had entered the world of benefits. It was to become a huge part of my life but I didn't know it at the time. Over the years with my increased confidence I have become a lot more knowledgeable about my rights and entitlements but at this time I applied only because it was suggested to me. I actually remember a few years after that, trying to claim the higher rate of DLA but I failed on at least two occasions. I remember filling the forms in by answering each question in a very positive way, making out that I was managing very well by myself even if I often needed help from my parents to do things. I didn't like accepting the fact that I was incapable of doing certain things. I guess I was still in denial. Following my diagnosis of ataxia a fellow ataxian and friend Greer helped me apply once more. She had been getting the higher rate for years and was similarly affected. She pointed out some home truths and got me to answer the questions similarly to which I had done before but in a slightly different way. I was no longer in denial. I was immediately put on the higher rate and have been ever since. This would have been in about 1995. I went to see the Citizens Advice Bureau when I was about to retire from work in 2002 to see whether I was entitled to any benefit when I medically retired from work. They told me I could get Incapacity Benefit to the tune of £400 a month, the benefit has changed name now but some 12 years on a quick calculation tells me that that is approaching £60,000 which would have been unclaimed if I had not visited CAB. This all goes to show I was coming to terms with my disability - in 1988 I applied only because it was suggested by my parents. In 1995 and 2002 I did it off my own back.

Despite not being truly comfortable with my physical condition or the diagnosis that was in place it should have been obvious to me that something was seriously wrong as every letter I had received in the past telling me of a hospital appointment jangled my nerves which meant sleepless nights for me. Try as I might to sweep my physical problems under the carpet, a feeling of doom I think was always with me, especially when people stared at me when I walked, which was hard to take. I knew it would always be this way. It depressed me when I thought of my mates with their girlfriends. Here was I with an incurable disease which always made me uncertain about my future. When I thought of my disease I knew I was never going to walk properly again. What made it worse was that I knew people were looking at me and so I would try to walk as best I could all the time, which took a lot of effort. I sometimes felt like I should have walked around with a sign on my back saying 'Don't stare! I have Charcot-Marie-Tooth disease' and also with a list of symptoms. I began to realise that I must truly acknowledge my disabled status and that I had to take charge of my life to make sure it was as positive as possible.

After some time of adjustment I did contact the CMT support group, which was my first stab at helping myself with some sort of background knowledge. This never felt right for me though. I never felt any sense of belonging and because of this I did nothing more than glance at the paperwork that was sent to me. I tried to get to know some people who had this CMT thing but corresponding by letter soon became boring and too time consuming - there being no email back then. After several years of a pretty dull life that I'd fallen into I realised that I must meet some people who had CMT 'perhaps they can show me how they cope with their lives' I thought. So the first thing I actively did after some years was to attend the Stoke on Trent CMT convention in August 1992. Before then my only concern was 'how would I cope with my life tomorrow'. Now though I realised that all my tomorrows would be the same unless I tackled CMT head on. I never felt for one minute that there was anything I could do to improve my physical abilities, it was all about sorting my head out.

Going back to my consultant I just want to say that I didn't really like him. I know I was young and facing an uncertain future but his emotional detachment did not help me or my family in dealing with my situation. He gave me a long list of standard questions, which didn't seem to refer to me at all. I seemed to be just a number in his book to him not a person at all. This attitude impacted negatively on my opinions about the medical profession for quite some time to come which was unfortunate. I was only 17 when I was seeing Dr Patten and didn't know how to react to people let alone be able to accept what he was telling me. I am an adult now but still, as a result of this initial contact with the NHS, cannot bring myself to talk about my future with medical professionals.

Ataxia

A whole five years after my CMT diagnosis, in August 1992 in Stoke on Trent at a CMT Convention I noticed that people there were moving around much more easily on crutches than me, which should have given me a clue I guess. I first heard mention of 'splints' when I was in an assessment workshop with 13 other people with CMT in the room, the leader of the workshop, a neurologist (a 'walking gait' specialist) wanted to examine each one of us, and as luck would have it he brought me up first. I couldn't get to him without using my crutches and immediately he suggested I did not have CMT at all and go to the National Hospital in Queens Square, London to get myself a re-diagnosis. 'I think it more likely you have multiple sclerosis or ataxia' he said. 'Oh no' I thought 'not multiple sclerosis' I'd never heard of ataxia.

After talking to the neurologist and looking back myself, it seemed to me that my earlier diagnosis had been made on a whim. The couple of days I'd spent in hospital doing EEG's and ECG's had obviously proved something was wrong but didn't make it clear to them exactly what it was. The actual diagnosis had been based solely on right to left eye movement exercises prescribed to diagnose CMT. - the so called 'medical profession' based a decision which would impact on me for the remainder of my life only on the slimmest of premises. This was an official diagnosis they said. They had told my parents, but I didn't believe it, not completely, call it wishful thinking or

71

a gut response. I actually had never liked Dr Patten, as I said before and in fact he left his post a couple of months after diagnosing me with CMT. Anyway the CMT diagnosis hadn't changed things for me as I probably would have not believed anything that was said to me when I was 18. I would still have been uncertain, miserable and lonely. A few years later after my ataxia diagnosis I had a tattoo displaying 'The Friedreich's Group and logo on my arm - it was a good job I hadn't tattooed CMT on my arm before that.

The formal diagnosis of Friedreich's Ataxia followed in early 1993 (8th January) at the National Hospital. It was, after all I had been through, a green light to make some positive changes to my life. Very soon after, I sat down with one of the ladies who worked in the office where I worked in Aldershot. I had worked there for years but had never spoken to anyone about my physical problems at all. I was using crutches to walk so my problems were apparent to everyone yet never had I uttered a word about why? how? or when? So for the first time I could speak to her about my condition and how it affected me, why it was there, when it started to develop etc., etc. I felt a change to my character - I felt immense freedom talking to everyone and I gained 100% in confidence. At this time too I stopped writing my diary. It had worked, it had done its job. The diagnosis also made me realise who I was. I suddenly knew what I wanted, knew my limits and felt comfortable with my body and mind. With the diagnosis I also gained a new circle of friends, and it is those friends who helped me cope with life.

In April 1993, mum, dad and I went to an Ataxia UK 'Talk-In' weekend, a few days designed to encourage ataxians and their families to talk openly about their experiences of ataxia. It was organised by Ataxia UK, formerly known as The Friedreich's Ataxia Group. Here I saw dad in tears for the second time. It was a real outpouring weekend. I remember it was the weekend that the Grand National was run falsely and was voided and also the FA Cup Semi-Final was between Sheffield Wednesday and Sheffield United. These latter things were what we as a family chose to talk more about than the Ataxia weekend, once we had all returned home - easier subjects I suppose. My parents had been there for only one day of the weekend but in this short time, I think my dad benefited more than mum and I did. Before that weekend if someone had said my dad would have cried in front of a load of people, I wouldn't have believed it.

For me the weekend was made bearable on two counts. 1) I fell in love that weekend with one of the girls who worked for the Ataxia group which was made even better as I stayed for the whole weekend, it was a truly independent time for me and evoked an outpouring of emotions and 2) from my memory, there were different workshops with different groups of people in. I saw people with ataxia, all of them wheelchair users, all more disabled than me, or at least I saw them this way. It was one of the first times I had used a wheelchair. I was pushed in a wheelchair by Michelle, the girl I had fallen in love with and for the first time in years I felt the air rushing over my cheeks. A sensation that all able bodied people just take for granted but for me made me feel so much freer. I found it possible to wheel myself around to speak to people and also no one seemed to be wondering what was wrong with me. Everyone understood, no one stared and that made the weekend exciting.

At this time I talked to mum for the first time about my 'problem'. I said I wanted to know who she had told and she told me - Pauline, Sandra, Jenny etc., she also told me that dad preferred not to talk about it. That is what I thought and somehow it felt good to hear mum say it.

I can still have times of depression about my situation and the disease, but on the whole I regard my ataxia as just part of me. In fact it makes me who I am. I simply live with the consequences of having the disease and with the annoyances, frustrations and embarrassments it throws up. Each of these emotions are caused by involuntary movements of my limbs, especially when I cough, sneeze or am startled. So when I am with other people it can cause extreme embarrassment, but when I am on my own I regard it more as an annoyance, a frustration or just an amusing event, depending on my mood at the time.

What helped in developing my current philosophy of life is the diagnosis of ataxia itself which has made it possible for me to solve problems in my life. It was like the previous years of uncertainty and worry evaporated. Overnight I realised that ataxia was not my own problem as there were other people who had gone through exactly the same things that I had. The physical problems I had with access is the massive change that the diagnosis brought to me. If before I had to climb five steps it was my problem, but with a definite diagnosis of ataxia it suddenly became society's problem and one which they had to address. I do get very impatient when I find something to improve my life, because despite having my own money to fund such things, it still takes time to organise people and equipment. I have to remember though that I am most fortunate to be financially stable.

Chapter 8.
My Family.

I don't think I felt any differently than any other child as I was growing up but having said that it is difficult for me to recall exactly how I felt back then. Looking back, I recall I was doing ordinary things as a child; playing football every weekend and going to school every day. I functioned normally within my extended family and was included in everything: visiting family members, grandparents and holidays etc. When I was younger my parents always provided a good and stable home, giving me things I wanted and needed, like food on the table, a taxi service, hospitality to my friends, holidays every year and Christmas presents. However, my sister and I have never really been given much emotional support from mum and dad. They have always been at hand to deal with life's practical issues, but not to offer much, if any, emotional support. It's just the way they are I guess, like so many people of their generation who grew up just having to get on with things. I might add here though that they have always treated me and my sister equally regarding this practical support. The everyday support they gave me back then included making drinks, meals and making sure I had clean clothes, all the stuff that it is normal for parents to do for their children. In addition, they were probably compensating for my obvious difficulties in my later teenage years, trying to make life as normal as possible. If I am honest though I spent a lot of time alone watching TV in my room, being on my computer and listening to music, fairly standard for many teenagers I suppose.

My parents definitely did the best they could for me; neither of them had much experience of physical disability before, other than from a distance with Catherine, my mother's cousin, who after contracting polio from an early age, was a wheelchair user. For instance, dad still never shares his feelings about me and the ataxia or much else to be honest, that's just him. My relationship with him wasn't helped by the fact that he used to hold out his arms all the time when I was transferring in and out of my wheelchair waiting for me to fall. It is natural I guess for a parent to want to protect their child, but I really didn't like that and still remember telling him so in no uncertain terms. As I mentioned earlier I did when I left home write them a *letter of appreciation* for all they had done for me and I want to say here and now that I still do appreciate their efforts on my behalf all those years ago. I am also always careful to thank them for the meals they provide for me now. As I mentioned earlier maybe dad's silence is clouded by sadness because he was sad and worried to see me leave home, but he could never bring himself to acknowledge that sadness and worry to me. In similar circumstances my niece has just passed her driving test and my sister has said that she feels upset because she will no longer be needed to drive her to places.

My extended family consisted of my grandparents Walter (Wally) and Rose on my dad's side and Peter (Pete) & Violet (Vi) on my mum's. Wally & Rose had 3 other children so I had two uncles (David & Roger) and one auntie (Sheila) from dad's side and one auntie (Pat) as mum's only sibling. These aunties and uncles produced 6 children of which my closest cousin was probably Ian, Roger's son. My paternal grandparents lived in Bracknell, a short drive away so I only ever saw them with my parents, but later on when I could drive I would see them by myself. My maternal grandparents lived in Bagshot, only a ten minute cycle ride away which meant I could see them more often.

With my maternal extended family we often holidayed together at Butlins just like millions of others at that time. These were fun times particularly memorable for the comical happenings that occurred there such as -

1.   *Grandad cooking us a meal and singing along to a track on the radio - he was singing 'bald headed woman'. I said to him its not bald headed woman but 'more than a woman.*

and

2. Another time was when I was 17 or 18 and at the camp with a school friend Alan, with whom I had just been out for the night. I was very unstable on my feet, nothing too exciting or what you might think! I remember we had gone to bed and I was woken up later by the sound of rushing water. It was dark, and I couldn't see clearly but Alan was standing in the corner of the room and was peeing. He had certainly had a lot more to drink than I! Being so shy I said nothing and soon went back to sleep. In the morning my sister and her friend Libby, both asked me why the towels which had been placed on the dryer in the corner of the room were so wet, I said the window was open and rain must have got in. I couldn't tell them what had really happened.

and......

3. One time with my cousin Austin, who was never the smartest cookie in the box but he desperately wanted to complain about the noise of people walking by the chalets when they had heels on. They used to click! clunk! all the way down the row. He was also annoyed about the size of the beds and he wanted to write something down that mentioned both those points. He wrote 'I am writing to complain about the noise of people's heels at night time because my feet stick out the bottom of the bed.' He was trying to talk about two different things, mixed up in one sentence. We had a good laugh about that.

Before either of my diagnoses I have to say I felt embarrassed about my condition because I knew nothing about it. As far as I was concerned there was nothing wrong with me, although some people just said I walked funny. However, without realising it at the time I was in fact not leading the life that a normal 18-23 year old should be living. In many cases a conventional young man would be talking to their parents about the usual problems in any young boy or man's life, but because my life had become far from what was ordinary I didn't talk to them at all. My illness as it began to develop was a taboo subject, to be swept under the carpet by everyone and especially my father. I talked to my parents about Chelsea Football Club instead, with nothing mentioned about my physical condition or emotions around it. I did not speak to them about anything at all concerning my health and well-being, which was a mistake in retrospect. My parents would have been to teacher's evenings when I was young but nothing was said about my problems and my failing sports prowess as far as I was aware. Anyway once I left school and was in my late teens, there was no one to ask as open evenings were a thing of the past.

On many occasions my mum particularly helped me out when I had small problems which were made much bigger by my worsening condition like the one detailed below,

'I put the ear drops in first this morning and then put my contact lenses in as well. There must have been some ear drops on my finger because when I put the lens in it stung like hell. So I removed it, put it back in its case and washed my hands. I then tried again - no difference. I took the lens out again quickly as it was very painful, but instead of putting it straight back in its case, I left it on the mirror. I wiped my eyes with a tissue, blew my nose and when I looked down it was gone. I called mum up and after 5 minutes she found it on the floor'

As my condition became more and more apparent, my place in the family changed because none of us, not even me consciously, realised what was happening. The change in the dynamic though was due to me, as I became insular and withdrawn. I was too frightened to talk about how I was feeling about having something going on with my body. If I was a young man now, things would have been different as it is possible to make a firm diagnosis for ataxia these days with better blood tests. When I went through my diagnosis, tests were done only on my walking and my gait. So you can imagine how I thought, I said "Thank God" when I finally received my correct diagnosis after waiting for so many years. This diagnosis, as you will know already, led to my removing myself from the family home as soon as possible, thereby effecting another change in family dynamics. The leaving was by no means escaping from my parents, rather for 2 other reasons 1. - I needed a wheelchair friendly home, theirs had stairs for a start and 2. - My sister, who is two years younger than me, had left home following her marriage 20 months earlier so I suppose I felt that I should leave too.

Perhaps as a result of leaving home and also because I have no wife or partner or indeed any children I don't really have a role in the family. My sister talks about things that would be called ordinary with my dad such as what her children are doing today or her day at work but when I am there the conversation dries up, it has always been that way or at least since we both 'fled the nest'. Now when we are having a family dinner I do feel quite left out and lonely. I don't seem to have much of an input because my life is not family orientated any more. As none of my family have had to deal with disability to themselves, they are always measured in what they say to me when they are with me, trying not to upset me or to say the wrong thing; something that they think may set me aside as being disabled or perhaps doing something that because I am disabled, I can't do.

Louise has recently had an accessible toilet added to her house. Obviously everyone can use it and importantly I can too. The toilet was set at the right height for me and rails were put on the walls where I needed them. When I went to Louise's to advise on this I was quite shocked that she had no idea where I needed the rails or where I needed to place my wheelchair to transfer to the toilet seat. I've been a wheelchair user 23 and a half years and not for one second has she considered how I cope with this necessity. It's an example of how my life has become so different to hers and why we don't have much in common. I am pleased though that she has had a disabled toilet fitted at her home so now I can stay there for longer if I'm invited. This makes me feel included in the family much more because I can be in their company at the house in comfort.

Children are so innocent they will ask anything that comes into their mind - they won't think about how the person they asked will feel or react so with Louise's children, it is different. Katie, my youngest niece, now 12, once asked how I put my shoes on. It's a perfectly natural question - here I am, sat in my wheelchair, unable to hold my own ankles in my hands so it shows a good enquiring mind. However, mum, dad or Louise have never asked me anything like this because maybe they think I would be embarrassed or ashamed to answer. When I answered she just accepted it and said 'Ah, I see' - no embarrassment ,no shame, no indignity. Just a simple question and a simple answer. I was actually quite pleased she asked.

Laura, Katie's elder sister being 17, falls right in the middle, neither an adult afraid of saying the wrong thing or an innocent child. I recently spoke to her about the fact that I was getting a new manual / power wheelchair (a life changing thing for me) her eyes glazed over and she couldn't leave the conversation quick enough. This highlights some of the difficulties I have - life-changing events for me mean very little to other family members. Perhaps that's why I end up just listening to what they do and hearing about all the things I missed out on in my late teens. Ages ago I do remember I spoke to mum and she said to me that she felt guilty about my having a disability from her and dad. I told her that she shouldn't as they had no idea that they were both carriers. They cannot be guilty of something they knew nothing about. So my silence aside I suppose guilt might be what has clammed them up.

A major example of overcoming problems thrown up by ataxia involves my and my family's passion, as Chelsea Football fans. As I have said before my first experience of watching the blues was in about 1976 when taken by my dad and I have had a season ticket now since 1987. Ataxia and the related mobility restrictions have obviously affected where in the ground I have been able to view the matches from. In my early teens I would stand in 'The Shed' (A covered terrace removed in the 1990's), as my ataxia progressed and my balance became worse in my late teens I began sitting to watch matches on 'the benches' (an area in front of the old West Stand, sort of an overspill from the Shed). My first season ticket coincided with my inability to walk unaided. I used to hold on to my dad's arm and 'clamber' to my seat at the back of the old West Stand. When a wheelchair became necessary for me, my family transferred our seats to the newer East Stand. I was able to get to my seat in the wheelchair and then transfer to my allocated seat at the back of the bottom tier of this stand.

Once, dad drove us to a Chelsea match, and unknown to either of us he had, when he was dismantling my wheelchair to fit it in the boot, left my backrest on the garden wall. We drove all the way to the ground before we realised what had happened, so without a second's hesitation my dad set off back home to get it while I sat on a wall and waited. I'm not sure this could be done now with the increased traffic on the roads. We missed only a few minutes of the game. This is an example that when it comes to life's practicalities. I could not wish for more understanding parents.

In 1994 transferring was becoming a problem but at the same time Chelsea were building a new North Stand, the Matthew Harding Stand, so I asked the then chairman Ken Bates, if a disabled balcony could be incorporated into this stand. To his enormous credit this was exactly what happened and I have been sitting there watching the games from my wheelchair ever since. The first full season there was 1995/96. So over the years I have watched games from all sides of the ground. I am now the disabled representative on the Chelsea fans forum and am coming to the end of my 2nd 2 year stint.

At Stamford Bridge in 2007 a great family uniting event occurred. It was the day that Jose Mourinho left Chelsea Football Club. 20th September 2007 which will go down in history... and not only because it was my 39th birthday! In fact the night before this Chelsea FC had invited me (as a serving fans forum member) with a PA, to a premier cinema viewing of a documentary outlining Jose Mourinho's highly successful first two seasons at Stamford Bridge. All the players were there except the captain, John Terry and vice-captain Frank Lampard. Owner, Chairman, Chief executive and Manager were also not present. Anyway, we got home late and I went straight to bed and was woken at 7am by the phone. It was my PA from the night before, Perry. 'Ah, that's nice' I thought - he's wishing me a happy birthday. The message he left on my answer machine was 'I suggest you watch Sky Sports News - Chelsea have sacked Mourinho'. We then knew why all the important people at the club were not at the cinema.

Also the previous year on Thursday 16th February 2006 Chelsea Football Club announced an intention to set up a Chelsea Disabled Supporters Association (CDSA) in order to improve the relationship between the club and its' disabled supporters. I subsequently applied to become a committee member and was selected a few weeks later. The formation of the CDSA was officially announced in a press conference at Stamford Bridge on 23th March 2006

I have a large collection of Chelsea programmes, as I touched on in the 'My Background' chapter and by the end of the 2012/13 season the collection consisted of 1690 programmes (plus 61 more on neutral grounds). Since World War 2, I now have the programme for every completed, competitive home match ever played by Chelsea's first team. I now also have all programmes for Chelsea matches played on a neutral ground too.

Our support of Chelsea FC, has always cemented us together as a family, and this culminated in us being named Family of the Season 2008/09. As an idea to improve and upgrade its museum, Chelsea FC invited applications from Season Ticket Holders to become the official Chelsea family of the year. A display of memorabilia and photos from that family would then be arranged by the entrance to the museum for all fans to see. Our family was selected from applications received from all over the world including Hong Kong and Australia. I gave the Club two 'season montage picture frames' that I had put together following the Clubs 04/05 Championship win and the 06/07 domestic cup double season. These were proudly displayed in the museum and were seen by approximately 100,000 fans during the season. This is something the family is very proud of. Our support runs back to the 1930's when my grandfather regularly attended matches. My dad then regularly watched Chelsea after the war and throughout the 1950's having been taken by his dad. He became a season ticket holder in 1962 when he became fed up with having to queue for tickets.

We also as a family were all invited to the launch of the upgraded museum on 25th September 2008 (co-incidentally the annual 'ataxia awareness day') and were interviewed by Chelsea TV and the matchday programme. I met two then current players namely Joe Cole and Carlo Cudicini as well as players from Chelsea's past i.e.: Roy Bentley, Teddy Maybank, Tommy Langley, Jason Cundy and Ken Monkou.

On Sunday 5th October, just over a week later than the museum launch, the family was presented on the pitch before the Aston Villa game with a voucher for £150 to be spent in a restaurant within the Stamford Bridge grounds and a shirt which had been signed by all the players. It was somewhat fitting that the presentation should be made by Ron 'Chopper' Harris who is not only Chelsea's highest ever appearance maker (795 appearances) but was Chelsea captain on my dad's most memorable day as a Chelsea fan: the day in April 1970 when Chelsea won the FA Cup for the first time. My dad was, of course, at Old Trafford that night.

The programme for that Aston Villa match featured a small write up and photo taken at the museum. You can see both this photo and a photo of us on the pitch in this book. [Pics 1&2]

The display in the museum reads:

'Introducing the Chelsea FC Family of the Season 2008-2009 - The Law Family. Pictured here at the '97 Cup Final: Louise, Terry, Pam and Matthew Law have been chosen as the Chelsea FC Family of the Season for 2008 - 09.

Terry Law, aged 74 has been supporting Chelsea since his father Wally took him to his first game, just after World War II and has been supporting Chelsea for 62 years. Growing up in Battersea with his two Chelsea supporting brothers, Terry has always been an avid fan. Holding a season ticket for 45 years, Terry is also a Chelsea PLC shareholder and Chelsea Pitch Owner.

He has passed on his passion for his beloved Chelsea to his whole family his wife Pam has been a season ticket holder for 44 years and daughter Louise brings her three blues-loving children at every opportunity. Their son Matthew has been a season ticket holder since 1982 and is also the representative for disabled members on the Chelsea fans forum.'

To be exact, it should have read that I was a season ticket holder since 1987 but season ticket holder or not I was going regularly in 1982 so I can see how they made the mistake. After our season as the Family of the Year the display was taken down in readiness for the next incumbents and we were asked if we wanted to keep the board with the official write-up on it. Dad obviously said 'yes please' and it is now on the wall at the back of a big cupboard in their home.

It is possible that my parents consider that my writing this book is a downer for them as they may be confronted by ways in which they could have done things differently. However, my intention in writing this book is not to point a finger at anyone but indeed to help other people with ataxia and their families to increase their options. Sometimes people have a view about disability as it is often a new situation to them and therefore can close down communication, if they are not willing to ask questions. It is still the same for my parents now so I hope this book will help answer some of the questions they have never asked.

When the family most needed emotional support I got all mine from Sue Grice, of The Friedreich's Ataxia Group (Ataxia UK as now) and not from mum and dad. Mum got a lot of support from Sue too. Never the twain did meet though. As with the hospitals, right up until the diagnosis of ataxia in January 1993, when I was 24, these conversations were held separately. As we, as a family, do not talk about the situation even now, I don't know what my parents were told originally. Information from the hospital was fed back to them and me but never together and this was a recipe for 'nothing to change' for the family. At least I have had an opportunity to say something to my mum but my dad even now cannot talk about it. We have never had a chance to start all over again which is a shame. I know they only wanted the best for me, to see me happy. I though, had my part to play in this conspiracy of silence too, as I would never come across as miserable to them. They never ever saw me upset. I would always try to hide the way I was feeling. With this in mind I do realise that if I presented a strong front this also prevented them from asking questions.

Because I always gave the impression of being completely unconcerned by my awkward walking, constant loss of balance, and declining sporting abilities as a teenager and young man I did not have the courage, nor in fact know-how, to seek the answers for myself. My parents seemed equally unconcerned; perhaps in part because I did everything I possibly could to hide my symptoms from them. For example, I would only walk down the stairs when they weren't watching or carry a drink when they were unlikely to see me. These tricks and games developed over time as things worsened for me. I guess if I seemed happy then they were happy.

The best way to get through this process of a worsening disability is for families to constantly talk to each other about how they are feeling. Everything stems from dialogue at the early stages. Asking more questions and speaking more is crucial. The ways I coped at school, like hiding my walking was sub-conscious and my parents have never known about it. Perhaps if I had told them about my worries back then it would have all been different and if I had been encouraged by them to talk more maybe we would have been a closer family now.

I think a vital problem for us as a family is the fact that our joint sense of humour has been lost since the onset of the disability. My ability to be a normal son to them has decreased as my disability has increased. Maybe if things had been different it would have been more humorous. Since my mid to late teens there has been a lot missing between me and my parents and there still is. I'd like them both to ask more questions about my disability and about how I feel about things but I do understand how difficult this must be for them.

Things could have been done differently but basically I didn't want to deal with it. I never spoke to my parents about my difficulties and I never talk to them now. It is a pattern I guess which with the passage of time is very difficult to break. I don't like to worry them. In hindsight I can say I would have liked it to be different. I compare myself with a friend Katie who has ataxia, which is more advanced with her. Her mum and dad knew about ataxia before she knew, she was just eight or nine years of age. They knew what was going to happen to her in the future, but for me that was different. I was an adult before I was diagnosed so confidentiality would kick in preventing my parents from being told about my condition without my consent. Maybe my mum and dad did not have that control over me as an adult, and as I said before I was never given information at the same time as them. Maybe they said to one another "We cannot interfere in Matthew's life now" and I wouldn't have wanted them to interfere anyway.

I am sure that my disability is something that doesn't sit easily with my dad. When I am with him and my sister at his home, it is highlighted to me how different my relationship with him is compared to Louise's. My relationship with my dad is not really what it would be if I wasn't disabled, I think. It's not a proper relationship but we have always got on fine and I cannot think of one single crossed word ever, well, in adulthood anyway! In Louise's company he is relaxed and cheerful; in mine he walks on eggshells and is always thoughtful about what he says not wanting to say the wrong thing. However, there are funny moments as a family such as when my sister was around for dinner just after one of the Bee Gees had died, we were discussing it and dad said "yes it's a tragedy really", Louise and I looked at each other with smiles on our faces and both burst into song 'Tragedy' by the Bee Gees. Granted, not too respectful I know but it was one of those moments.

After all these years I still don't think my dad can come to terms with his son having a disability. When out with his friends, I would imagine that my disability is a subject he always avoids. He would talk about me, possibly even my wheelchair but never the difficulties around it. He would talk about the fact that I go to foreign football games, I am writing a book, and I live on my own but the Friedreich's Ataxia would never enter the conversation. Mum is different, she has lots of friends that she talks to about me, and it doesn't faze her at all. With my sister it is very difficult, I rarely speak to Louise about stuff. She came around to see me years ago when her relationship with Lee had broken down and asked me what I felt. I suggested she draw a line under the situation and move on, but she didn't seem to like that, I guess because of the feelings she still had for Lee. With Louise It has been pretty much like it has been with dad but for different reasons entirely. Louise has her own life, three kids, a fiancé and a job as a teacher, she is busy doing her own stuff.

Both my grandfathers served in the Army and both played a role in the Second World War. My dad's dad served in the 42nd Battalion Royal Tank Corps and mum's dad served in the Kings Royal Rifle Corps. All my grandparents are no longer with us but I do remember my mum's dad Pete, saying to me, when he found out that I was going to hospital for tests, he said "I am sure it is only a storm in a teacup". He thought it would all go away. My dad's mum had Alzheimer's disease for many years before she died in 1997 and my paternal grandfather was totally blind due to glaucoma when he died four years later. Twenty years ago I wasn't too noticeably disabled anyway so it never really came up with them. I have no relationship with my cousins now and apart from the one with my cousin Ian, when I was a small boy I did not have a close relationship ever really.

All my four grandparents died between their 85th and 92nd birthdays and I do think about a time when my parents are no longer around. My mum is ten years younger than my dad so it follows that I'll probably lose my dad first but of course no-one knows what's going to happen. Both are in very good health at the moment. If my mum dies before my dad, I'm not so sure how my dad would cope on his own. There are so many things he cannot do. I do worry about him. If dad dies first mum would be fine - she has loads of friends and would deal with life's day to day challenges without a problem. I would obviously miss them dearly if they were no longer around but I do not think their deaths will affect me in any significant life-changing way. I do see them every weekend and every Friday I go round their house and have dinner with them. I would have a steep change of weekly routine that would take some getting used to however. My relationship with my sister would change, I hope. I do not get to spend any time with my sister at all these days sadly, due, I guess just too leading totally different lifestyles. Maybe I would see more of her. However, even when we were both living with mum and dad we never really had a close relationship.

Although not seeing much of my sister [Pic 35], my relationship with her and her family is fine. I am not really close to any one person in the family in particular. The people I am truly closest to are other people who have ataxia, they are rather like an additional family that provides me with emotional support, which has been lacking in my biological family. I got very close to one of my first girlfriends Donna, a fellow ataxian. I enjoyed sharing with her all the things I had not spoken to my parents about. I now feel close to my friend Katie and a few others with ataxia. When I was at the 'Talk-In' weekend, with Ataxia UK back in 1993, for the first time in my life I felt totally at ease with who I was. My parents were there too of course, but I felt instantly much closer to the people there who had ataxia; everyone had a link to ataxia and knew why I was in a wheelchair. Everyone knew about my wobbles. This left me free to be myself. I guess this feeling has remained with me over the years.

Perhaps to reinforce the past cultural issues that may have underpinned my close family's response to my condition I recount here a story from my aunt, who has kindly agreed to break her silence on the tragic loss of her son and the trauma that has occurred for his twin brother, occasioned both by her and her family's inability to cope and the lack of true support for families back then.

'Mark and his identical twin brother, Austen, were born on the 21st August 1966, both happy, healthy babies, but Mark lived for just 4 months and died suddenly, a cot death - something that could so easily have been prevented.

For me, as his mother, it was firstly utter disbelief that this could have happened, then despair and self-blame – I should have been more careful; I should have checked on him sooner, why didn't I realise something was wrong, etc.

I sank into depression and it was also a difficult time for Roger, the twins' father. I felt unable to care for baby Austen without panic and anxiety and it was decided that he would be cared for by his grandparents. At that time, the 60's, there was no counselling available and the attitude was that this was something I just had to get over and move on with my life. After several months I was admitted to hospital where I had various forms of treatment for depression and I attempted suicide, feeling responsible for Mark's death and my total failure as a mother and as a wife. When Austen eventually came to live with us again he was one year old. Mark's death had filled me with fear and anxiety which prevented me, in many ways, from experiencing with Austen the natural enjoyment that mothers have from seeing their child grow and develop.

It is my deepest regret that Mark did not get to experience a life which he could have shared with his twin brother and his family, making friends, learning about the world – all of those experiences which make up our lives. Regret, too, that Austen did not have his brother around to share his life with. Also, regret that, because of this tragic event over 40 years ago, I have missed the opportunity of having a relationship with my son, Mark.

There is always, for me, the knowledge that it could have been so different if I had admitted that I was struggling to cope and if I had asked for help during those first few months after the twins were born. I believe that there is now far more professional help available to new mothers and I would urge them to ask for that help as soon as they feel worried or anxious, and to check on their babies as often as they feel necessary to reassure themselves that all is well.

These words are so indicative of the ways in which my own and I assume many more families dealt with the knowledge that a child in the family had a disability or would die suddenly. The issue of my family's response to my condition does require a response on my part. After all this time I still do not know if my dad feels disappointment in, embarrassment about or pity for me. It is difficult to know or even gauge. He may be proud of me but never tells me. I watched a film called "Sunshine on Leith", sort of a story linking together lyrics from Proclaimers songs. In one part of the film a soldier with lost limbs was asked about his dad's reaction to his son's disability, he simply says that they only talk about the weather. This struck a chord with me as I recognised the relationship between father and son. My mum is totally different but when they are both with me it is awkward because I cannot speak so freely and nor can mum. When we are alone we can speak about anything, which is good. Because ataxia is an elephant in the room when I am with dad.

In hindsight and for me, I think any emotional support from any quarter would have been useful. If dad had become more involved in the Friedreich's Ataxia Group; because my mum was involved, they may have been able to share knowledge together. As a family no one knew what anyone else knew, which meant no one could support anyone through it. The simple fact was that dad just would not ask questions and mum did not want to go against what he wanted.

Pic.1.Taken at the launch night of an upgraded Chelsea Museum at Stamford Bridge on 25/09/08.
Joe Cole presents the 'Family of the Year 08/09' Engraved plate to my dad.

In Pic: (l to r) Joe Cole, Carlo Cudicini, dad, David Law, Stuart Law and me in front).

Pic.2. Before a home match with Aston Villa on 5th October 2008 the Law family was presented with a signed Chelsea Shirt (for being family of the year 08/09) by Chelsea's record appearance maker Ron 'Chopper' Harris.

In Pic (l to r) Ron Harris, Lee Perry, Terry Law (dad) Claire Forrester , David Law, Joe Perry, Pam Law (mum), Laura Perry, Katie Perry, Louise Perry, David Harris (my pa for the day), me in front.

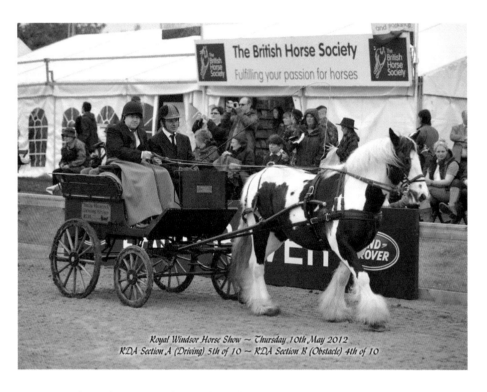

Royal Windsor Horse Show ~ Thursday 10th May 2012
RDA Section A (Driving) 5th of 10 ~ RDA Section B (Obstacle) 4th of 10

Pic.3. Royal Windsor Horse Show - Thursday 10th May 2012. Riding for the Disabled Section (RDA).

Pic.4. Royal Windsor Horse Show 10/05/12
I receive my award for finishing 4th from the Duke of Edinburgh.

Pic.5. Me, Donna, Sian (standing) & Mel about to leave for a day at Sha Tin Racecourse in Hong Kong on Saturday 22nd October 94.

Pic.6. I went to a gym once a week in Frimley Green, Surrey between 2003 & 2011.

Pic.7. Me, John Ebbs, Sain Rhys and Donna Smith at one of many fundraising events held at Donna's parents' house in Acton Turville. Picture taken in 1994.

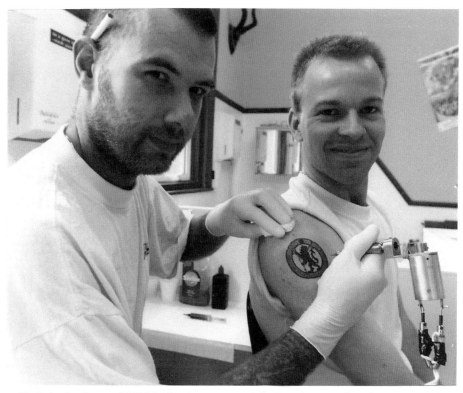

Pic.8. I raised over £1500 by having a tattoo inked at the top of each arm. My left arm has 'The Friedreich's Ataxia Group inked on it. My right arm (as shown) has the classic Chelsea FC emblem. I had these done on my 25th birthday in North Camp near Farnborough.

Pic.9. Sat in the gardens of a restaurant in Gothenburg, Sweden in May 1993. This was in my first ever wheelchair - called a Meteor.

Pic.10. Sat with Melanie Preston by the Dead Sea in Israel in December 1995.

Pic.11. Another fundraising event. A parachute jump in August 1995 raised another £1500 for the then Friedreich's Ataxia Group. Now Ataxia UK. A video was taken of the jump. This photo shows 16 images taken from the video.

Pic.12. May 2000 in front of the old Wembley Stadium on FA Cup Final day.
Chelsea beat Aston Villa 1-0. Within 6 months the stadium had been demolished.

Pic.13. I'd just won Butlins Bognor Regis 'boy of the week' at table tennis.
Aug 80 (aged 11). I'm pictured with an England Table Tennis Coach .

Pic.14. Having just done my parachute Jump (skydive). Aug 95.

Pic.15. Kim Wilde and me at the opening of a Restaurant in Aug 93. The profits from the restaurant would go to FAG (Ataxia UK as now) Kim Wilde was, and still is a patron of Ataxia UK.

Pic.16. Me with Liz Lowry 2001.

Pic.17. July 98. In a rare day out from the office, all the Civilian Staff at 145 Brigade were invited to attend the Reserve Forces Exhibition. I am pictured here just before a trip out on a raft with my bosses boss Eric.

Pic.18. My life between the ages of 22 and 24 was lived using crutches to walk. This was maybe the most difficult time of my life so far. I hadn't even considered using a wheelchair then. Here is a rare photo of me at this time pictured next to my dad at my sisters wedding (June 92).

Pic.19. On a Glass Bottomed Boat above the Great Barrier Reef, just off the coast of Cairns, Australia. June 99.

Pic.20. Chelsea had just won the FA Cup in May 1997. My sister, dad, me and my mum celebrate in the car park at Wembley.

Pic.21. Probably the last time I ever wore a bow tie! This was taken just before I left for an fundraising event arranged by the Friedreich's Ataxia Group in May 94 .

Pic.22. I was a good footballer as a young boy. This is a photo of my team (Curley
Park Rangers) when we were in the Under 10 age group.
Pictured (l to r Standing): Me, Keith Harmes, Andy Inglis, Andrew Southerland,
Gary Lovett, Jason Bilston, Anthony Connelly
(Kneeling): Lloyd Cornwall, David Carroll, David Parker, Shawn Kelly, Craig Logan,
Mark Kirkland, Richard Leverentz.

Pic.23. At the Curley Park Rangers U11 presentation night.
Pictured: standing l to r David Parker, Gary Lovett, Jason Bilston, Craig Logan,
Andrew Southerland, Mark Kirkland, Andy Inglis
kneeling Keith Harmes, me, Shawn Kelly, Graham Johnson, Lloyd Cornwall.

Pic.24. In the summer of 2002 my friend Miranda came over from Australia with her husband and 2 young daughters. Miranda has Friedreich's Ataxia and has written several books about her travels round the world. This photo was taken on a day out at Legoland.

Pic.25. Meeting a koala in Marapana Wildlife Park, Perth, Australia. July 1999.

Pic.26. Playing in a football match for Curley Park Rangers U12s.

Pic.27. Taken in my sister's back garden in 2003.

Pic.28. A rare picture of me in my late teens.

Pic.29. Outside Wembley in May 2000 with my sister, Louise. We were about to watch the last FA Cup final played at the Stadium. Chelsea 1 Aston Villa 0!

Pic.30. Me when I was 2 on the back patio of the house where I grew up (Gloucester Road, Bagshot)

Pic. 31. Me when I was 4 on a family holiday in the Isle of Wight.

Pic.32. In my parents back garden, aged about 8 (1976/77) .

Pic.33. Me when I was 10 on our first family holiday abroad in Majorca. We used to holiday each year with a local family 'The Balcombes' This was our first holiday with them.

Pic.34. Me when I was 11 on our 2nd holiday abroad in Minorca. Again my dad was the photographer and again it was a holiday with 'The Balcombes'

Pic.35.My sister and me.

Chapter 9.
My friends and my school life.

Through my secondary school days I gave up each sport in turn and over time, first football, then cricket, after that table tennis and golf, and finally I gave up snooker. Each time I stopped playing a sport I had a sense of relief. I did not give them up because I could not play them at all, but because I found it frustrating that I wasn't as good as I once was. Snooker was maybe not quite like this. Each of the others had become physically difficult, but with my snooker it was more about my balance and walking than actually playing. So with the first 4 sports there was absolutely no mourning for what had been lost; in fact I was pleased that I gave up playing because I wasn't enjoying it. I did mourn the loss of playing snooker though and maybe I am still mourning it to some degree. Snooker was my last way of competing on equal terms. I still miss the competition which I only find now in Fantasy Football League although I have fundamentally lost the competitive emotion.

My teachers at school never made any comments about me and my worsening condition even those who would have noticed i.e. my sports teachers. I had no conversations with any of them at any time, and I now know from mum that she was never approached by a teacher either. In the teachers' defence, I suppose they were mostly employed to improve my brain only and in all lessons I sat down so no teacher would notice my physical issues anyway. As for the games teachers, I'm not so sure why they would have remained silent. Maybe they suspected something serious was happening to me, not least because at the age of 10 or 11 I was one of the best at all sports and by the age of 15 I was one of the worst. However, there was, back then, no imperative to note each child's development in quite the same way that children are monitored now. Things have totally changed over time at schools. Teachers must now note down the development of all children and even games teachers must have to do the same.

Of course if they had asked me or my parents something, I or they, wouldn't have known anyway and because of that I in particular would have made light of any questions that were asked. As I was once a 'star pupil' in Games groups, it is likely that I encouraged the teachers, through my obvious embarrassment, not to publicise their thoughts anyway. I do remember one of our games activities was swimming. One example of how I managed to manipulate situations to my advantage was with the school swimming activity. Walking in bare feet round a swimming pool on slippery, wet tiles would have been impossible for me and would certainly have raised questions about my walking abilities. Somehow though, I managed to get myself promoted from D Group to C Group when it was D Group's turn for swimming.

A friend is someone that you have common ground with and someone you can relate to and who knows about your being and how you function. A friend is someone you can speak to about feelings and emotions. Friends generally are important to stop you hiding away by experiencing things together. However, I wouldn't say friends are the 'be all and end all'. I can in fact, without any problem, spend a day or so at home without any outside contact. It is not a desperate urge in me to have friends and I am far from craving friendships but having said that I do like it when someone new comes along.

Friends make you feel good and when you have things to say they listen and share your life. It is good to have people in your life when you have something important to say. When I am feeling down I like to be able to talk to someone because this often makes me feel better and not alone. I have a lot of friends on Facebook although only either fellow ataxians or friends I have made outside of Facebook. If I don't know who sends me a friend request then unless I know they have ataxia I will not accept their request, as this does not make them a friend in my book. I see a friend as someone you can relate to on a one to one basis.

With hindsight, I realise that things were more difficult for me than for my peers at school, but at the time I was in total denial that I was in the least bit different to anyone else. My peers may have begun to notice a change in me when I was about 12, but the changes I was myself experiencing, were slow and incremental. My school friends would have been the first to notice these I guess as they saw me the most, although I would always do my very best to hide any problems I was having because I didn't want to be considered different from anyone else. Ironically, the best way to hide my worsening physical condition was to maintain the level and range of the sports I already played. Surprisingly when I ran, the problem of my mobility was not so noticeable initially. The main difference particularly to others was in the way I walked because walking takes more balance whereas running takes its force from forward momentum.

Having said all that I was just like all my peers in other ways, I was a bit of a joker and got into all sorts of scrapes especially with my friend Graham. One particular story comes to mind which I am sure many early teenage people will recognise. It focusses on an English lesson discussing poetry, when we were about 12 or maybe 13 -

Teacher *'A poem needs to be planned out and thought through before being composed'*

Me *'I'm sure we could make one up on the spot'*

Teacher *'I'd be interested to hear you try'*

Me *'OK, me and Graham [a good classmate who was sitting next to me] will do one now'*

Teacher *'OK, make a poem up using the Topic title 'Fire'*

Me *'OK - Fire is red'*

Graham *'Fire is hot'*

Me *'Oh yes it is'*

Graham *'Oh no its not'*

Me and Graham laughed so much we were both sent out of the classroom to recover. This is a classic example of ordinary teenage bravado.

I remember at school I used to dread the bell ringing to signify the end of a lesson because that meant I had to walk to my next lesson - with my friends of course! I would do anything I could to avoid walking with them. I learnt many tricks over the years: I would ask the teacher a question after the bell went so he would still be answering me as everyone else left - but of course I would need to pretend to be interested in the answer; I would go to the toilet and arrange to meet my friends at the classroom where my next lesson was; I would do my shoe laces up as everyone else left the classroom or be the last to walk down the stairs - and always walk very slowly. I tried all of these tricks just to stop my mates noticing that my walking was not as smooth as theirs. Similarly, when riding a bicycle I had no problems, but to grind to a halt at traffic lights or a road junction would mean having to stop and balance the bike by resting my foot on the ground. This would cause me balance problems so to avoid being asked questions about it, I would make sure I lagged behind the group or stormed off in front.

As a young boy (Maybe 10 or 11) I used to go swimming with Graham over at Bracknell Sports Centre. His mum used to take us and the car journeys over there were always more memorable than the reason for going (the swimming). Graham, his mum and myself got into the habit of singing 'Mahna Mahna' (if you're not sure about this song, google it) on our way to and from the Sports centre. It wouldn't be for just a few minutes either. It was for the whole journey. We had such fun. Happy days!

I must say the main thing that resulted from these tricks was a lack of deep friendships, as I tended to miss out on the general banter between my closer friends and in larger groups when walking or riding my bike. Of course at the time I felt I was doing the right thing because I was preventing any potentially embarrassing situations. I viewed my disability and its attendant awkward walking and constant loss of balance as an annoyance, a frustration and a massive embarrassment. I was ashamed of myself and felt so mortified that I found it easier to stay 'shut in' my bedroom than to see everyone and face questions that I didn't know how to answer. Of course now, I can see that this was not the right way to deal with it. I should have gone out there, faced people, spoken to my parents about how I was always losing my balance and tried to find out why and what was happening to my body.

Things I did for fun - I spent hours and hours every week kicking a sponge ball around in my bedroom with Graham. We would take it in turns to go in goal. The goal was just a large map of the world on the wall behind the bed. The goalkeeper would dive around on the bed trying to stop the ball from hitting the map. The striker would kick the ball from various places on the carpeted bedroom floor.

Between the ages of 12 & 15 my only thoughts were about getting through the day. I was having the same education as everyone else and so as I was not missing out on anything and I just got on with my life and continued doing all that I wanted to. I regarded my loss of sporting abilities as simply 'the way it is'. Like millions of schoolboys I was not going to be good enough at football to be a professional - no big deal! As I didn't know the reasons for my declining health, my friends were unlikely to know either. They were probably aware that things weren't right but even when they brought the subject up I could not give them any answers because I didn't know myself. It was as if there was a huge wall in front of me and I found it easier to hide behind it than attempt to break it down. To be honest, as I progressed through my teens, my friendships dwindled away as I became introverted and more and more afraid to discuss my feelings for fear of being asked questions that I couldn't answer. The friends I had, dealt with things much like myself - they just accepted me for the way I was and got on with things. For the most part before my diagnosis this didn't impact too much as all of us were on the cusp of manhood, but not yet. This meant that during the seven year delay in diagnosis I was not pitied by anyone nor could they sympathise with me because they, like me, didn't know the truth. I was fortunate too that I experienced no real bullying because of my condition. I suppose there may have been a lot of discussion behind my back and there were one or two sniggers to my face. I think that 'Has he been drinking?' would have been the worst and most common comment that was made.

A bit older, maybe 15 or 16 we [me and Graham again] were at Bracknell

Sports centre playing snooker. Our friends Richard and Andy were playing on the next table up. Richard was a good player but always thought he was much better than that. He would stand and cue as per the textbook always making sure he looked professional. He left himself awkwardly positioned when striking the cue ball for one particular shot. He was stretching awkwardly over the table trying to strike the cue ball with his shoe just touching the floor (as is legally required). As he cued his foot slipped and his chin quickly followed by his chest and arms collapsed on the pile of red balls gathered around the pink spot. The balls went all over the table and it was a source of amusement for me and Graham for weeks.

University or College were never really an option for me. I would have just told my parents that it wouldn't have benefitted me or that I wasn't clever enough or some other story. The truth though was that I simply would not have coped physically with a change of environment nor emotionally with a change of friendships. So I stayed on at the same school in what they called 6th form college. I can see now that this provided an ideal smoke screen to stop me contemplating my future. It enabled me to keep some friendships because a few of my friends did the same and stayed on for a further two years to get some 'A' levels. I made a few new friends as well like Paul who you would have read about in the My PA's Chapter.

Upon leaving this college at 18 I began to feel extremely lonely and isolated as all of my peers were finding employment and even more importantly were getting relationships. There was no ball or event to mark the end of our school or 6th form days and it is unlikely that I would have gone anyway, but this did not help me in sustaining what few friends I did have. It meant that people often drifted away as they do after school when their new university or working life kicks in. Nowadays, the thought of a school reunion would frighten me as my hearing would make it very difficult to interact with anyone. It was easier back then to just hide myself away from my friends and from life in general. I figured that once I was employed, like my school friends, I would simply go to work and also go to all the Chelsea football home matches with mum and dad. That would be my life. I had no social life - hence my decision to spend my time writing a diary, discussed in detail in the next chapter. Like most people you go in different directions in life unless you make the effort to keep in touch. I felt though that I was trapped with this dread problem, which made it too difficult to be out in the world, even though I wanted to be.

Maybe 15 or 16 years of age playing the well-known board game Trivial Pursuit, a hilarious incident involving pronunciation occurred when reading out the questions. About 5 or 6 of us were playing - and Graham was reading out one of the questions: 'Who released their debut song in 1967 entitled 'A witter shade of pall'. Everyone was totally confused and said they'd never heard of it. Then I realised he meant 'Whiter shade of pale'. He felt embarrassed, we just laughed. Later in the same game I read out the question 'Who was the famous 1880 bushranger' only instead of 'Ranger' I could have sworn it was pronounced 'Rang er'. The embarrassment was all mine this time. Again, the others just fell about.

A few friends did remain with me beyond my schooldays. They were people I had things in common with like football or snooker. I had friends from my local neighbourhood who when I gave up football, played snooker with me, and they stayed friends until I stopped playing snooker. These friendships though were built around snooker and once that stopped there was little left to keep us together. Also the fact that I was becoming disabled may have subconsciously led me to pull away and emotionally detach myself from everyone in my past. Luckily I went off to work fairly soon after leaving school and I got work friends without having to hark back to schooldays and the mates I had had then. Work just got in the way, so it wasn't a conscious decision to leave them behind.

'We went to play snooker today, mainly because Neil, Richard and Andy thought they would get a drink out of me, no way! Somehow I always feel that I am being left out by them and even on this day I still felt that way.'

I do see Graham, a former neighbour and school friend fairly regularly. We used to play football together and he stayed a friend even when I removed myself from everyone else. We were very close at school as we both played up front at football, both scoring goals and there existed a rivalry between us. Maybe he felt he owed me a friendship as I felt I did him. Graham was especially aware about the deterioration in my health and he could see what was happening to me. However, we never talk about it, how I might be feeling or the future prognosis, I am not too concerned anyway, and don't feel like raising the subject, but wonder what he thinks sometimes. I am sure he and others get embarrassed about asking questions for whatever reason. Also my dad and his dad are still really good friends. He now lives and works down in Southampton. His life is not all that structured so he turns up with little warning and usually one of my PAs is here so it is less easy to chat about things with him, so we don't talk about anything too deep. Also, I usually get a couple of emails from old work friends at Xmas. One has retired recently so she will have more time to come and see me, I hope.

'I had a roll and did some more stats homework and just waited until 1.05pm, then it was Info.Tech. until 2.25pm and after that I sat on the field with a group of boys - but still I felt lonely and left out. Again I sat doing nothing and talking to no one for 40 minutes and then I walked over to Kingston on my own to get a lift back home - what a day! When I got home I felt like crying and probably would have done if I was on my own.'

Following my first diagnosis I made a couple of friendships, through the CMT Support Group, with others who were affected, but our symptoms never really seemed the same, and, as we didn't seem to have similar problems, nothing came of the friendships. I do remember though going with one such friend to the Aston Villa Leisure Centre in July 1991 to see Transvision Vamp, a pop group whose lead singer was Wendy James. The CMT support group also provided me with information that I then used to find out about the CMT convention in Stoke on Trent in August 1992, which changed the course of my life. It is just a shame that if I had been braver and more honest earlier, with my family and friends because then, I would have got to see a doctor sooner and that would have led to an earlier diagnosis of ataxia instead of waiting until I was 24.

In 1992 I had begun to realise that I wasn't living my life correctly, although as early as 1988 I had become conscious of my friends all leaving home and I began to wish for that too. Finally, with my ataxia diagnosis in 1993 I had all the answers. Independence could be achieved. Holidays abroad started and I moved in to my own pad and as a result I gained many new friends and even some acquaintances became friends, almost overnight as I felt more confident talking to people. Most of my friends now have got ataxia and I use Facebook to keep in touch with them. My lip reading teacher who is helping me to better function in noisy social settings says she uses Facebook because it doesn't matter if you have hearing or other problems. I must admit I agree with her as my limited ability to visit people regularly impacts on the way in which I can maintain friendships.

My friend Katie who I mentioned earlier to her enormous credit has set up a local support group for people with ataxia. Katie lives in Coventry, about a two hour drive north of here. I agreed to go up there and see her when she had her first meeting and was invited as the 'guest speaker' for the second. It was never my intention to join this group as a member but I enjoyed the first two meetings and so decided to become a member. Fairly regularly I attend these meetings but I am dependent on a PA being free to drive me there. These meetings have enabled me to make new friends, and some are now friends on Facebook too. I would regard Katie as a close friend. We met ten years ago because we were both put on the same leaflet for Ataxia UK, I read the leaflet and I read about her and she seemed to have similar interests to me. We got in touch by email and the rest has just happened from there. We have been to Spain and Cyprus together as part of a group holiday.

Given the accessible nature of my housing estate, I also have neighbours who have disabilities and who have become friends. Darren, Peter, Chris and of course Justin, who I used to go to school with. Our mums played bowls together, that is how mum found out about his ataxia and after that we got in touch with each other. I heard he was applying to the council for housing and at the time both places either side of my house were empty. He asked me which would be the best for him to live in so I made a suggestion and he moved in. We now pop into each other's houses sometimes and we even watch the odd football match together. He has a ramp at the back of his house, so access is great for me although once my back wheel came off the ramp and I got stuck, so he had to call the paramedics to help me! We can obviously get to each other's houses ourselves using our power chairs. It is always by arrangement though, as neither of us like the doorbell ringing and being unready to receive someone and cater for them. There are other places too where I have acquired some friends over time and these are my trips to Chelsea matches and over at the horse riding stables which I attend regularly.

My main friends now though are, it is true to say, my PAs. Paul, who was a school friend, mentioned before, is more like a friend than a PA, and most of my PAs I regard as friends first and PAs second. Interestingly enough I do not regard my latest PA as a friend. I don't think we click all that well, we have more of a carer / client relationship as I discussed in the 'My PA's chapter' regarding Grace, but she does everything I want her to do and is reliable. This is not a bad thing for me in a way, as these days I find it easier to deal with. This is because making a friendship with a PA and then seeing them go feels like you are losing a friend more than anything else and it has happened to me too often. Friendships develop, especially as I see people for 12 hours a week and having a person in my house means this is an obvious outcome.

Generally I have not had troubles with boundaries whilst PAs have worked for me. However, when a PA wants to leave when I don't want them to, I have to just get on with it. A person left recently and I had to take her off Facebook as I used to read all about her stuff, especially her opinion that she had done the best thing in moving onto a different job. This hurt me. I emailed her to tell her why I took her off after she queried why I had done it. I told her I missed her and I didn't want to be constantly reminded. I explained and she understood. Interestingly, she did a sponsored run for Ataxia UK last November and so we remained in touch arranging that. It felt good for me to help her to get sponsorship forms, and an 'I support Ataxia UK' t-shirt to run in and to advise her on how to go about raising money. She raised aver £1000 too so we did something right!

For all aspects of my life especially friendships I would be at an absolute loss without the internet. I depend on the internet, for shopping, banking, payroll, research, for everything really. The internet is my lifeline. I don't speak to people every day using it but it is good to know it is there. For instance I haven't spoken to Justin for over a week and he lives next door. Particularly in the winter the internet comes into its own, but I do tend to find I am more active socially outside the home in the summer. I generally like being out more. I am quite busy in the summer. In winter my view is 'turn your lights on and sit with your feet up' and with the internet it makes some socialising possible.

I would like to make new friends and there is no reason why I cannot. I am comfortable either with people who have ataxia or with people with an interest in sport. I struggle to make conversation otherwise. There is also an online forum on the Ataxia UK website but I prefer to make my own contacts.

Chapter 10.

My Diaries.

'It's 2 weeks now since I started writing and I am still going - can't be bad.'

'Why on earth should I start to write a diary today? I've been thinking about it for several weeks but I kept refusing myself because I was thinking it was just whenever I felt down that I wanted to write and that didn't seem right.'

'There's no way I'm going to be able to write every day. What I'm going to have to do is get a diary and just write in it when I feel like it, even if it is just once a week'

I started writing my diaries at the age of seventeen, when I was working for my exams and a working life was looming. Like so many diaries written by young people, trying to come to terms with the world as a teenager at the beginning of their adult life, the main and often negative focus was my angst. In my case, this was a terrible foreboding about my deteriorating physical condition and how it affected all other areas of my life. At first, these feelings put me off as I had before that time been a happy-go-lucky kind of person and the thought of writing a diary seemed negative. The early weeks and months of my diary writing focussed on the first diagnosis of CMT I received before my ataxia one, my learning to drive and my first relationship, so this proved that diary writing could involve both good and bad things.

'I am sitting here now, December 2, 1987 and listening to my first ever compact disc.'

I started writing the diary because, given that since the age of 12 many changes had occurred in my physical body, I felt as though I needed some way of communicating my feelings with someone. Also things were developing technologically as mentioned above and it seemed to be a good place to talk about things that interested me.

'I still don't know if writing a diary is a good thing or not; whilst it enables me to get my problems off my chest, there is no way my diary can sit down and talk my problems over with me and in fact I am no closer to solving the issues I have than before I wrote.'

As I have mentioned before, talking directly to another person about what I was going through was simply not an option for me. Lots of people have good friends or family they can talk with, but because I was so embarrassed about and humiliated by my condition, I couldn't. Of course like many people when I had a good day I was not so inclined to write but when I had a really bad or a boring day my diary was a real comfort. It had its limitations though as you can see from the entry above, the diary was not a real person but an interface only; it was much more actually 'virtual' than many online chat rooms like Skype or MSN are now.

'There are 4 things I really want at the moment and they are 1. A girlfriend, 2. A car, 3. A job and 4. Jimmy White to win the Embassy World Professional Snooker Championship. At the moment it is the latter 'want' that seems most likely to happen.'

I guess most of my peers would be talking to a mate about a relationship breakdown, but not me. I wrote it all down, addressed or kind of 'spoken' to my diary, which in itself was a start but with hindsight nowhere near as good as getting some friendly feedback. For me at the time though it was a means of getting out how I was feeling and it was always 'like' a sort of support mechanism. I felt much better about my life if I had written how I felt in my diary.

'I have a hell of a lot to say and a hell of a lot of time to say it in because I

finished with Andrea last night.'

I was not at all aware of other diarists, historical or contemporary, so when I first started I probably didn't know what I was doing. As time passed I became more and more comfortable with writing and I loved the discipline and the comfort of writing a daily diary, usually in the evening after my dinner. We had never even been asked to write anything even approximating to a diary at school. I know that other people who attended different schools were asked to write a diary about their summer holidays, but not us. Also before I started writing the diaries, my English was appalling at school, but by the time my diary writing career had ended I had improved markedly. In that respect it did me good, as well as being a means to make sense of my world. I'd never had the inclination to write until fears and anxieties were beginning to bubble up inside me due to my deteriorating physical condition.

'I've just realised that I get depressed when I'm bored and have nothing to do, i.e. my mind is not occupied and so I am continually thinking of the future (and the present) which, at this moment does not offer much, to say the least.'

If I am being honest I am not a diarist; by that I mean someone who knows they are writing for an audience. These abound now with the introduction of the internet and the diary form called blogging. However, I am a man who wrote a diary, that is all and for me I never thought anyone would read my diaries, and particularly I never wrote the diary with publication in mind. I thought I would be dead before the diaries were read. This enabled me to be confident in sharing my feelings in the diary because I knew it didn't matter what I wrote because no one would be reading them anyway. This meant that it was so good to express the way I was feeling without holding back.

'I'll write in 2 parts tonight "I'll write now, before Jasper Carrot, about what has happened in the last 2 days and then later about what has happened

inside my head.'

The day to day **minutiae** entries like the one above, may not be for everyone, but my diaries did record important events in my life too and these have been skilfully transferred into much of this book. Having said that, the boring day to day stuff does show exactly how limiting my life was because I had a very restricted social and personal life through all those years. This I think serves as a timely reminder to people not to bottle up their feelings if they think something is wrong, but to talk to people, as well as write things down if they find this a useful tool.

'Before today I had never considered leaving home but I sometimes wonder if it would be best if I made a fresh start somewhere else. I really do feel that my life is not progressing while I stay here. I am losing all my self-confidence and although my parents try to make me feel happy, I know within me that I am not. I could create a new image for myself and start from scratch. Ken Dyne the fourth member of our snooker team got me thinking of my future life. He did a 4 year course at Edinburgh University and he now works for a computer firm in Camberley.'

When I first started writing the diary I thought it might be a phase. I thought I would write a little bit every day, that is all. I didn't realise what a major thing it was going to be in my life for the next 7 years. I gave the amount of time it took to writing a diary no thought whatsoever and I wrote a page a day normally. I knew unconsciously it was the right thing to do and the regularity of it kept me grounded through very difficult times.

'Tonight is just one of those nights when I am not in the mood for writing. Nothing interesting, exciting or depressing has happened over the last couple of days so I have no real reason to write but that will change on April 7th for that will be one year since I started writing my diary. After this date I will only write when I have good reason to.'

When things were going well in my life I may have felt enough was enough sometimes, and even gave up writing for a while but then something bad or difficult happened in my life and I would go back to it.

'This is the 2nd time I have written today. This morning was full of hope and anticipation but now most of that hope has gone and it has left me feeling rather empty and it seems with nothing much to look forward to.'

Eventually though as things proceeded in my life and with the developing ataxia I didn't feel complete unless I had made an entry of some kind.

Instead of writing as though I was creating a novel or short story, I decided that the best way to do the diary was for me to address the diary as though sending a letter each day to a friend. I don't think I could have carried on just writing down my events of the day. It would have become a biography otherwise, which was not my intention. I would address each entry as *Dear Diary* and sign off as *Matthew*. For me this gave the diary more of a purpose, making it more personal and as if I was sharing my life with someone. The diary became a kind of surrogate friend. It functioned as my best friend and someone to tell everything to. **Never did I think I would, aged 43, give my diaries to someone to transcribe them before I set out to write this, my autobiography.**

My parents knew I was writing something of course. I never actually discussed it with them but they knew it was a diary. At 9 o'clock every evening I used to say I am going to write my diary. I would have thought they would have been interested in what their son was writing about, but I trusted them to know that what I was writing was not to be read by anyone, especially them. I never in fact discussed the diary with anyone else outside. I simply did not have that kind of relationship with anyone - if I had, I would not have needed my diary. My parents certainly had the opportunity to look at it but I don't believe they did. I trusted them so much that I left the diary on the floor down below my desk. I never remember having to deliberately hide it, unlike other teenagers who have complex locks on theirs and hide them in a locked drawer or a safe box.

'It took me a long time to write what I did this morning, I was concentrating hard until Louise came in at 12.05. I was then only writing for half the time as I had to make sure she didn't come in when I was writing. I had the TSB application form nearby and pretended to be writing that when she came in.'

As I said before, when I was happy I rarely wrote anything in the diary and also when or if the diary became difficult I stopped writing it. Once I stopped the diary after my ataxia diagnosis I never wanted to go back to it. I viewed it as a part of life that was closed. Never did I want to lose the friend completely before my diagnosis though. The diagnosis was the life changing thing for me. At last I could speak to a 'real' and not a 'virtual' person about how I felt.

'I haven't written for ages and there are 2 main reasons. 1. I am losing interest and can't be bothered most of the time and 2. When I AM in the mood something comes up and I have no time.'

I was also busy from the time of my ataxia diagnosis, sorting out my wheelchair and my new house. In effect I had an excitement rush then and I felt my life before this time had been wasted years. Only since then have I lived the life I was meant to live and started to make up for those lost years. There was simply no place for diary writing when life beckoned instead. Of course another reason may have been my deteriorating handwriting.

So the diary writing had had a shaky start, I didn't know where it was going to take me or even if it would be a long term practice. It turned out to be quite a few years in the making but it stopped much more definitely and immediately than it had started.

'I am quite pleased that I have not written over the weekend. I have plenty to write about but I have resisted the temptation. Besides, as I have said, I

have had a lot on my plate.'

I guess with all new things, the beginning is delicate as you step into the unknown, but ending things can be sudden, which for me occurred in 1993. Since that time I had not looked back at the diaries at all, but interestingly enough they are now living again in this book so I must have done something good back then. Some of the things that have come out of my diaries being read by someone else and then written about in this book have been a revelation to me. Indeed some things I have no memory of at all, which I guess is no surprise for a couple of reasons: a) I wrote the diaries 30 years ago and b) I wrote the diaries as a means to counsel myself and as such they were written when I was emotionally in a difficult place, thereby making them somehow, *'over there'* and no longer a part of me. I just dumped my feelings on the page, so to speak.

I don't think about my diaries at all now except as the role they have in this book. After this book is written I know I should put them back on the shelf where they will stay. Having said that they could be used for medical research when I am dead and gone. They might be good for a medical researcher to look for signs of ataxia or other complaints, and from there to develop appropriate support mechanisms and strategies. Other people might benefit from knowing, because there must still be loads of people out there who have lived or are living the same sort of life as me, before my diagnosis. For instance, a good friend of mine, a fellow ataxian I got to know around ten years ago, I asked "Before you were diagnosed, how did you cope with knowing something was wrong?" she said I just got on with my life, and kept busy which was exactly my view before I was diagnosed and is exactly my viewpoint now.

Chapter 11.

My Relationships.

'I decided long ago,

never to walk in anyone's shadow

If I fail, if I succeed

At least I live as I believe

No matter what they take from me

They can't take away my dignity

Because the greatest love of all

Is happening to me

I found the greatest love of all

Inside of me

The greatest love of all

Is easy to achieve

Learning to love yourself

It is the greatest love of all'

'*The Greatest Love of All*', Whitney Houston 1984

The song lyrics quoted above are poignant for me though I believe that one can only start to love oneself when you know there is someone who takes you for who you are, which I had felt my first girlfriend Andrea did at the start of our relationship. Before her, I hated myself, but since knowing her I came to accept myself for who I was. Despite all that went on between us, and the way that our bust up affected me emotionally, I do have her to thank for the beginnings of my self-confidence.

'I went to Thorpe Park yesterday with Lee and Louise, but was alone all day. They did their best to make me feel welcome but I had constant reminders of my loneliness, seeing couples walking arm in arm everywhere.'

My first proper relationship with anyone occurred from when I was 24. Only at that time after my Friedreich's Ataxia diagnosis and having had an abortive first love in my late teens, could I love myself, now knowing who I was and what I wanted out of a relationship. This enabled me to give others a chance to love me. Relationships for me are about companionship and friendship within a mutual sexual attraction and coupled with support. I also see it as a way to build a life together over time.

'It was then that I learnt that I may never see Kate Fairly again. She has got one exam on Monday, one on Tuesday and then on Wednesday she starts her new job. It just goes to prove my point that if you are attractive or handsome, you stand a better chance of getting a job than if you are not. It makes no difference how many 'O' or 'A' levels you've got, all you've got to be is good looking. Kate is just another girl who I fancied, got to know, thought and dreamt about and who has left my life without me doing anything about getting to know her more intimately.'

'I hope to God this disease doesn't get no worse! How will I ever get a girlfriend if I appear weak and feeble to everyone?'

I started having a relationship with Andrea Parson's back in 1987 when I was 19. I have Friday 7th August 1987 etched into my brain: the day I first asked her out and she said 'YES'. I was extremely nervous, so much so that I couldn't eat and felt very sick at the thought of a) asking her out and b) being rejected. She agreed to meet me in Reading the next day. I was a bit surprised as she said "Don't come to the house, let's meet outside somewhere." I was very excited and yet couldn't stop wondering what she saw in me? I guess all teenagers feel the same unless they are totally sure of themselves and confident with it. The next day though was a disaster, which

I can probably put down to nerves. I set off for Reading and got there quite quickly, but could I find a parking place? Erm........no, I could not so at 2.30 I left Reading without seeing Andrea. I got back at 3.30pm after a 9 mile detour due to being lost and I called Andrea's house straightaway. She of course was still in Reading waiting for me. The next day having gone around to meet her mum, we went to Windsor Great Park, where we had a walk around and shared our first passionate moment. No, we didn't scare the horses..... this was just a kiss! This was to be one of many mainly chaste moments, grabbed between our parents being around and the return of the parents of children we were babysitting. I still felt terrific though holding her in my arms for hours.

Things were going quite well generally though despite a few niggles, a major one of which was my football training. I was assistant manager of an under 10's boys team at the time; I'd given up playing by then. These coaching sessions got in the way of my relationship and my ability to be with Andrea for meals etc. She never seemed very pleased to come second to my passion for football, or snooker for that matter. Some of these niggles led to Andrea sometimes not phoning me when she said she would, meaning I didn't get to see her, because in those days before mobiles we only had landlines to work with. If you had to go out, then you missed calls. My patience began to wear thin and I slowly realised that she wanted me because I had a car and could ferry her about. I would not have minded this but to then be faced with a lack of affection on her part was very upsetting to me and I began to feel used. I was very confused that suddenly she didn't want me to touch her. I couldn't understand this change of heart coming so quickly after our first date.

'Love is the most important thing in life and when it doesn't come your way, you don't feel as if it is worth living.'

My disability also meant I couldn't and also wouldn't go to things like discos, which Andrea liked to do. This was because having tried discos I now hated them because the flashing lights, drunk people and the loud music, let alone the expectation that I should dance was just too much for my wobbly legs and my deteriorating hearing. Over time I noticed that the gaps between seeing Andrea grew larger and larger, and when I did see her she was less and less affectionate. I was beginning to feel the first pangs of unhappiness after having been so ecstatic for the first few weeks, especially the first one. I had been so proud and happy at that time, but many apparent misunderstandings occurred as the weeks went on and it is easy now with hindsight to assume that they were full of purpose on her part. She was perhaps trying to force my hand and get me to leave her.

I really needed Andrea after my car accident, which occurred some two and half months after we had started our relationship. This had left my face black and blue and I wanted her to care for me. I was worried though that the sight of me would put her off; this was to be a test of her love in my eyes. When we did meet, she would not even hold my hand. I don't think she realised that just being around her was not enough for me. I felt after such a long time together I still hardly knew who she was. Andrea was four years younger than me and she had been a person who made me feel wanted and a four year age difference shouldn't be too much but at certain stages in life it can be frustrating and difficult. This was the case with Andrea who I often felt to be too young, and quite naturally as a result was not wishing to rush into a full - on relationship. This was my first love, and I was like my peers with their girlfriends, proud to have her on my arm. It was like finally I knew that there would be someone else in my life. Or so I thought. Looking back on it, having this relationship was all consuming for me - I would think about her all the time, about how I felt and also the little things that happened between us.

I think my disability also had an impact on her, because I didn't know what was wrong with me at the time and it was a taboo subject between us. I only have had meaningful relationships since the diagnosis of ataxia when I could then talk about my feelings, but back then at the age of 19, I didn't know that was possible for me. Everything was a secret locked inside of me. Andrea also never asked me questions. I think she must have viewed that her boyfriend just walked a bit funny and that is all. I got on with her parents but not that well. I guess they could see that there was something wrong with me and that must have worried them. I can remember her dad but not her mum. I thought he was a bit of a strange bloke. He behaved and talked strangely, so much so that I could never sit down and talk to him about anything, which I suppose at that time was par for the course for me.

Towards the end of our relationship I knew that I had to have a heart to heart with her but I just could not bring myself to do it, despite knowing that if I lost her because of my lack of communication I would never forgive myself. I was beginning to feel like I would never get a girlfriend if it didn't work out with Andrea. I knew it wasn't right for a girlfriend not to want to hold hands or kiss and I felt resentful and confused about being put in the position of having to raise the issue. When I had asked her about it before she had a list of lame excuses, not least that she didn't like kissing someone in their bedroom (which had not stopped her on the first night we went out together). This all made me feel terribly unwanted, foolish and sad and reflected back to me how I felt my world was, in the context of my worsening physical condition and the way other people viewed me.

'My sister and I's last night on our own then - mum and dad will be back at about 6 o'clock tomorrow. So I will no longer have the car to myself. I have enjoyed the last two weeks - I like the independence and I like not having anyone telling me what to do and when.'

Approaching the end of the relationship I began to feel like it was my fault and that as she was so young she may have felt out of her depth with me and also with the prospect of a serious relationship. After a few more weeks of missed phone calls and disappointments I began to feel like there was more to her behaviour than met the eye. She seemed almost scared of me now. I was in a Catch 22 position now because I needed to tell her about my physical condition, but I couldn't risk that until I knew she loved me. However, as she seemed to be losing interest in me and would not even respond when I told her I loved her, the writing was on the wall. I began to avoid her, as I actually preferred to play snooker than see her, as it at least made me happy, which she was not doing at that time. This carried on for a little while and on the 28th November, some three plus months after we first went out, I finished our relationship, after picking her up from her nan's for the umpteenth time, a ritual I was really fed up with. She didn't argue with me either, which was hurtful and it was also clear she did not want to talk things through. So I was alone again and I dared not even think what would happen for me next.

Once I finished with Andrea I felt very lonely and left out. I had invested so much in my relationship with her and I had begun in my own mind to make plans for our future together. So it was a shock to realise that she was not making those same conclusions in *her* head. One of my thoughts was 'why were people getting partners and not me?' People might say "Plenty more fish in the sea" but for me I already knew that my chances of finding someone long term were narrowing as the years went on and my disability began to show itself. As well as my peers getting girlfriends this more often than not also resulted in my friendships stopping with them when their relationships began. This then was the time I was withdrawing from society, I was too self-conscious and embarrassed to go out and having people asking me questions about my walking etc. I found it easier to sit indoors and to write my diary and do things with mum and dad or visit predominantly male dominated arenas like the snooker club. Anyway, even if there had there been any girls at the club I wouldn't have felt confident to approach them. My confidence then was just about as low as it could get.

'I thought back to when my dad told me the worst years of his life were between the ages of 24-28. I then asked him what changed his life at 28 and his answer was obvious - he met mum and got married. If I have to wait 10 years until I meet someone I would be driven insane I am sure.'

My low confidence and self-esteem were to undergo another dramatic and positive shift when my diagnosis of ataxia in 1993 was confirmed. Many people would think a diagnosis of a degenerative disability would be the end of a normal life but for me knowing what was wrong with me was like a breath of fresh air, one which would from now on enable me to talk to people without the fear of being unable to explain my physical issues. My three serious friendships with women after this involved Sian, Donna and Mel who were women I was put in touch with by Sue Grice of Ataxia UK

148

after I had a chat with her about how lonely I was. Donna was my first girlfriend with ataxia, after my diagnosis, we became very close and we spent a great deal of time together. Towards the end of 1994 I would spend every other weekend with her at her parents' house, just off junction 18 of the M4 in a small village called Acton Turville. Donna's parents, Sally and John, had made their house all wheelchair friendly and as I was still getting used to being a wheelchair user I thoroughly enjoyed the freedom we both had in their house. Naturally ataxia was the dominating force in the relationship and we used to talk a lot about our lives and feelings around it. She was the first person I could relate to emotionally and physically. Looking back now the time I spent with Donna at her parents' house was amongst the happiest of my life [Pic 7]. I really liked Sally and John too and was always made to feel just like a family member when I was there. As Donna had been diagnosed with ataxia as a young girl, the whole family were very experienced with all things disability related and so it is easy to see why I enjoyed being in their company so much.

Whilst there on one occasion we decided to use the rather impressive swimming pool that her dad had built her some years back. Donna was a strong swimmer and used to spend many hours in the pool swimming and exercising muscles that the buoyancy of the water made possible. I was never a keen swimmer but I had learnt many years before and surely it would be like riding a bike - once you've done it, you always can - right? Wrong! There were several small points that had slipped my mind. 1. I'd not been near water for at least 10 years, 2. I had ataxia which meant (amongst other things) that I could no longer walk let alone swim. 3. Donna was a regular and experienced swimmer. So in blissful ignorance I climbed down the steps using the expertly placed handrails straight from my wheelchair and pushed away from the side of the pool to join Donna in the centre. Within 2 seconds I was floundering around in the water, fighting for my breath and thinking that my time was nigh. After what seemed like an hour of struggling to breathe my airway unblocked and I was at the other end of the pool with Donnas arm around my back.

Donna had just saved my life and at the same time had prevented the need for either her brother or her mum, who were at this time watching with horrified expressions on their faces from the side of the pool, from jumping in fully clothed to rescue me. Whilst Donna and I were together, she met an able bodied man and decided that he could give her what she craved in terms of love, security and support. All good things come to an end I guess!

Sian was the very first person I met with ataxia. She lived at the time with her parents in Ascot, Berkshire, and a fifteen minute drive away from me. I never had a personal relationship with her but we have always been friends and have never fallen out. She remains a good friend today and someone I meet regularly at the horses at Merrist Wood. We also see each-other occasionally when either of us has a PA to drive us to the other's house.

Mel and I visited Israel in 1995 on a Winged Fellowship trip. The Fellowship was a religious group, but I went along to see the sights as I am not into religion myself. Mel sadly died in 1998, from a severe stroke; we were very close and we had been boyfriend and girlfriend for a couple of months, a while before this. She was very attractive, so much so that I was more attracted to her than Donna but interestingly I got on better with Donna. Mel lived in Nottingham and because of that we didn't see each other much, only about once a month in fact. On the night before Mel's stroke, she rang me and as I was in the shower, I didn't pick up. I heard her message and I thought I would ring her the next day. It is a big regret. I went to Mel's funeral, and a friend from work called John also came along as he knew her from a holiday we'd all been on in Tenerife four years before. It was a huge shock. I remember going up to see her in the Queens Hospital in Nottingham, two weeks after her stroke and seeing her laying in a coma and she looked asleep to me. She had breathing apparatus on her and I said to her dad, "When she wakes up will you tell her I came to see her?" The way he looked at me made me realise she was not going to recover and it really hit me then.

I originally properly met and spent time with all three women by inviting them all to join me on a trip to Hong Kong in 1994, which is mentioned at length in the My Travels chapter. This was the first holiday I attended which specifically catered for disabled people. The thought of Donna as someone I could be romantically involved with developed on this trip. We did, over time, become just as close as two people could be.

I was friends with Liz [Pic 16] for a few years before we became close in any way. She had been on the Hong Kong trip too in 1994 as a helper. She was not directly employed by the organisers, Surrey Phab, but I think her trip was subsidised by them, in other words, she was there to help and that is what she did - helped everyone. She pushed wheelchairs, provided a steadying arm to some of the ambulant disabled, helped feed people who couldn't feed themselves, helped people in the bathroom or helped people to bed. She was vastly experienced with persons with all types of disability and knew many of the people that went. She was friendly and pleasant and got on with everyone, regarding everyone as an equal whether fellow staff members or the disabled clients.

In the days before I could employ PA's I needed friends like Liz who was not fazed at all by being out with and supporting disabled people. We did many things together like doing my weekly shop at Sainsbury's. Without her my life would have been unmanageable, I'd gained the confidence to start living a 'normal' life but I needed support and Liz provided it. I was fortunate to have her. One day in November 96 I treated her to a day in Blackburn. It just so happened that Chelsea were playing there that day (Zola's debut, 1-1). As we were leaving for our overnight stop at a nearby hotel, my car broke down. The AA toed us to our hotel where we stayed until the morning, before they drove us back home in a big truck with my car on the back on the Sunday. Me and Liz got to know each other really well on this weekend and became close. We were sort of 'secret boyfriend/girlfriend' at this time. I'm still not sure who knew and who didn't but I think we both preferred it that way. This 'secret relationship' lasted a few months until we both realised we worked better as just friends.

The fact that over the next ten years she travelled as both a friend and a PA to New York & Orlando in 97, Australia in 99, Canada in 99/2000, Toulouse in 2000, Scotland in 2001, Grado (Italy) in 2003 and Cyprus in 2005 is evidence that we made the right decision. Liz now lives a distance away with her 2 children aged 7 & 5 and their father. We are still friends but circumstances for both of us make it difficult for us to see each other.

My next girlfriend was Victoria from Swindon. It was now 2007 so I had been waiting quite a while. Once again in a twist of fate I met her for the first time in Reading, how bizarre is that? She has both ataxia and dystonia, a kind of movement disorder and uses a wheelchair. I first laid eyes on her at an ataxia conference (I'm always a bit braver in this company) and we got to exchanging mobile numbers. I had invited her to my house for dinner and as Swindon and Reading are both connected by the First Great Western line out of Paddington, it seemed a good idea to pick her up from Reading in my car. I remember we first kissed on my sofa here. It was only immediately after this that she told me that she had a boyfriend already, which was a bit of a shock. Within a couple of weeks she had split from this boyfriend and was with me for about 4 months. In this 4 months I had planned a holiday for us (and 2 PA's) in Portugal the following May. The first thing that crossed my mind when we split up was what would we do about the holiday? In the end we decided to go as just friends and this actually proved to be emotionally easier than I thought it would be. I learnt to forget all about the feelings I once had for her.

It has been some years since my last girlfriend and I would like a relationship at the moment of course, if one were to come along, but I feel I am happier without anyone rather than being with someone who is not right for me. In my experience of relationships I feel 'as high as a kite' when I'm in one and devastated when it ends. So I consider that not being in one makes my life easier to manage. No highs, no lows just an equilibrium. Having said that, I don't feel I have achieved what I want to in life without a relationship, but the practicalities are difficult. I do not mind my own company and I don't need the constant chatter. It is not something I would draw a line under and say it is not going to happen ever but I feel closest to people with ataxia, so this limits my chances somewhat and two wheelchairs would not work in this house. If I was to live with another wheelchair user we would have to move somewhere else.

Conversely, I would not feel comfortable with someone who didn't have ataxia, as they could never understand what it is like to live my life. But you never know! One of the friends I have who lives in Australia, called Miranda [Pic 26], is married to Mick who is able bodied and they have 2 happy, healthy girls. Over time I think it is fair to say that she has become more physically dependent on him, and I am pretty sure this is because she has someone to do stuff for her. I think this happened for Donna too. She found someone to depend on. When they split up she needed 24 hour care. This situation also plays a part in my thinking about relationships. I am sure a partner would *want* to help, they would love you and support you but I would want to do it myself.

Relationships to me are made more complicated by my disability and how I deal with it. I always want and need to do everything (within reason) myself and having another person in my life would mean that would change. In my case I would have to move if I had a relationship which for me, given the efforts to which I have gone to ensure a good life in my present home, would take an immense leap of faith and a new unlooked for start to new adaptations involving lots of hard work.

Chapter 12.

My working life.

During my time with Andrea I had worked for a Children's Activity Centre for children aged 11-16 during the school Summer holidays. I got a small hourly wage and expenses and led games like rounders and cricket. One incident sticks out in my mind from that time which brought my problem into sharp focus as characterized in this diary entry -

'Up until today no one had the faintest idea about my disease. They maybe thought I walked funny but they did not know there was something wrong with me. Until today, I had not had to run - I just played backstop or bowler - so that I would not have to. Margaret (the site-leader) decided that we would have a staff versus children match - this meant I had to run - and fast - round the bases. I hit the ball very well - every time (probably as well as anyone had hit all last week). But my running was embarrassing. I was unbalanced and found it really hard. In the end, someone offered to run for me. They obviously saw the problems I was having and saw how tired I was. I was grateful to them but at the same time I was embarrassed at having a runner - what could I tell the kids as they shouted out - what's wrong with him?'

My working life spanned 1987 to 2002 and listed below are the various jobs I have had which I will talk about in more detail in this chapter -

21/12/87 - 23/09/88 Royal Army Chaplains Department, Bagshot Park

26/09/88 - 24/08/90 Army School of Mechanical Transport, Deepcut

28/08/90 - 02/04/93 41 Squadron (Sqn), Aldershot. Mons Barracks (Bks)

05/04/93 - 23/02/96 41 Sqn, Aldershot. Gale Bks

26/02/96 - 29/08/97 145 Brigade (Bde) Aldershot

01/09/97 - 20/12/02 145 Bde Aldershot as an employee of Sodexho

I never talked to my parents about my career ambitions; they always wanted me to do what I wanted. However, my first job lasted only for about two weeks and was a rubbishy job, just feeding paper into a machine. I never talked to my teachers either about my ambitions, because at that age you never really think what you are going to do with the rest of your life. However, I knew deep down there was something wrong with me which meant I would not be a professional footballer or a rock climber. I already knew my limitations and I decided I needed a desk job.

'It's funny but I am not nervous about the actual interview, but I am about what to wear and how I have to get there.'

I remember at school we all had appointments with a careers advisor. I just had one meeting though. I did this because everyone else met with her, so I didn't want to be the odd one out. I must also have been to a jobcentre but I cannot really remember those sessions. I applied for loads of jobs and I was particularly interested in a career in banking as in my school days I had been always interested in figures and maths, which I still am. I got loads of letters returned to me saying 'unfortunately we do not have an opening right now'.

'For the first time today I realised just how hard it is going to be to get a good, satisfactory job.'

Mum was instrumental in getting me my first proper job. She knew someone at the Post Office where she worked. She asked this lady if she knew of any jobs going. As luck would have it she did know of an administrative assistant's job going at Bagshot Park Army Chaplains Department. Their office was close to where my parents lived which was a five minute drive away, so it was perfect for me. I used to play cricket on the pitch in the surrounding grounds when I was younger so it was all familiar to me. I had no idea what I would be doing when I got there, but to be honest, I was ready for almost anything: work was such a necessity for me if I was to approximate to the life my peers enjoyed. My CMT (ultimately in fact my ataxia) had been diagnosed by then, and was presenting itself as my just being very wobbly at that time, so the fact that the job was based upstairs didn't cause too many problems. When I was walking up and down any stairs at that age I needed a handrail, I was relieved that the office stairway had one.

It was not difficult to get the job either, and the fact of my being local made me an ideal candidate for both my employers and myself. I had the minimum 5 O'Levels, and this thankfully did at least put me on the bottom rung for employment. I didn't have much of an interview. I think I just turned up on 21st December 1987, as things were much less formal back then. I started working and after three days we broke up for Christmas. My main duties were to answer the switchboard telephone, deal with incoming and outgoing post and filing. This job was probationary, indeed it was a temporary civil servant post. If I had been no good they could have got rid of me. As it turned out, all of my time there was probationary before moving onto another job.

By contrast, for my second job at Deepcut, because I had to be inducted into the civil service properly, I did a lot of research to support me in the interview and I do remember thinking that I am going to need to know what the civil service, MOD, the job and the army were all about and as a naive 19 year old I had no idea so I looked it all up (In books - no internet then!). By the time my interview came round I was actually quite confident. The interview was held in what is now a health centre, but back then the MOD Smith Doreen House stood there. Thankfully, they asked questions that I had researched and they actually let me know about a week or ten days afterwards that I had the job. For the first time ever someone made a serious comment about my disability during the interview. As the CMT diagnosis was in place, which I mentioned earlier, one of the panel said "What is this tooth disease you have?" Somewhat stunned I replied "It has nothing to do with my teeth at all, it has something to do with the way I walk." I felt really quite humiliated to be honest. I didn't appreciate anyone talking about my lack of balance or my wobbling. They didn't however ask how they could help me or support me so it did seem like a pointless question. I imagine things would be different now, following equality legislation and increased awareness, but during my time at Deepcut, the only thing I myself was able to do to assist myself in accessing the building was to park my car close to the road that I had to cross to get there. This would avoid a lengthy walk to the office which would increase the chance of stumbling or falling but it wasn't always possible.

At Gale Bks, some small changes had been made to accommodate me on my crutches. For instance, I used to park my car close to the building and use my crutches to get from the car to the door. When I later began using a wheelchair, of which more later, it would stay by the door all night and be waiting when I arrived in the morning. I was allocated a particular parking space which was the one adjacent to the pathway approaching the entrance. I also got unofficial assistance from a work colleague to hold the heavy fire door open and hold my wheelchair as I sat in it. Eventually I stopped using my crutches and this work colleague (John Ebbs) would bring the chair out to the car. Also I think all the inner doors were fire doors, which had shutting mechanisms, making it very difficult for me, so they took them off. Maybe they should not have done that because it was against health and safety. Unfortunately, I did just have to cope as best I could in the loos as they were individual cubicles. I would just leave my chair outside the cubicle and 'stumble' in as there was no disabled toilet back then. Thankfully my mobility was not as bad then as it is now.

Throughout my early working life my colleagues must have wondered about my lack of balance, awkward walking and frequent stumbles but kept it to themselves. It was very difficult for me because I still couldn't speak to anyone about it, I had been diagnosed with CMT but I didn't know anything about it. I blocked any questions being asked because I still had nothing to tell them. I did get a bit of light hearted teasing sometimes, and once in the canteen at 41 Sqn in Mons Bks, I lost my balance and fell over by someone's feet. This female colleague said "I've never had men diving at my feet before and its quite nice" I was embarrassed and because I didn't know any better I used to grin and laugh with it.

I must admit that each job I got was better than the last one in that each was more specialised and more interesting for me. I enjoyed working at Bagshot Park and I got on very well with everyone. The work was fairly standard and nothing too taxing. I also liked the work and people at Deepcut, although the parking was a fair distance from the building and across a - all be it very quiet - road. I acutely remember the worry I had as I walked - stumbled - up to this road crossing. I was fine if the road was clear as it was 90% of the time: my forward movement would provide the balance I needed to stay on my feet. However, if there was a car coming and I had to stop I was in trouble as I didn't have the required balance to remain still on my feet. I had a good view of the cars on this road as it was long, straight and unobscured. I could tell, shortly after taking my hand off my own parked car and beginning my 'walk', if there was a car coming along the road. I would adjust the speed of my 'walk' so I didn't have to stop. I would speed up to get across the road before the car got there or slow down to allow the car to pass first. I was at Deepcut for two years and only messed this up a couple of times. I became quite an expert at changing direction and walking along the path - in the same or opposite direction as the car so as to avoid stopping. On the occasions that I messed it up, I would go down and tried to hide the fact that I'd actually fallen. I would do my shoelace up or pretend I was picking something up that I had dropped.

Once inside the building I had to negotiate a flight of stairs like I'd had to do at Bagshot, which as things were getting more difficult for me physically, became a struggle. I do remember one of the parts of the job at this driver training establishment was to record all the details of the soldiers that enrolled for the driver training. At the beginning of their course they would wait in a queue for this to be done. My job was to write everything down - computers were beginning to appear - but not yet for us. I would write everything in a massive log book; names, regimental numbers, unit, date of birth etc., etc. and I used to really hate that, everyone was waiting for me to write things out. It was a pressure and I really struggled trying to make my writing legible and I used to feel harassed. It was only once a week on a Monday. We would enrol only about a dozen soldiers a week but I used to dread Monday mornings for that reason. I am pretty sure that the soldiers would have talked about me and the slowness of my writing. Interestingly, we had a small machine in my office that could detect if the soldiers were colour blind or not. I would operate the machine and ask them to peer into it asking them what they can see. They must also have wondered if I was an optometrist! I don't think a civil servant would be allowed to do that these days!

In 1993 due to Army restructuring and improvements 41 Sqn was moved from Mons Bks to the brand new Gale Bks. As the crow flies this was only about 400 yards but it worried me because I would have a whole new set of physical challenges to work through. At Mons Bks I had begun to use crutches to aid my balance as my walking had become too much of a problem and falling had become too frequent. It was just before 41 Sqn's relocation to Gale Bks that I was diagnosed with ataxia so I knew things had to change for me. I started using a wheelchair there. At this time every one of my work colleagues noticed a change in me and my personality, for the first time they began to see the real me. Within a few months I was approached by the Officer Commanding, who asked why I had changed so much - he knew I had begun using a wheelchair at work during this period. But couldn't understand why I had gained confidence and become happier and more talkative. I agreed to type out a whole page answering his question, but I never did find out what he used this for! Maybe as part of an inspiring speech he was giving! Who knows? When I started using a wheelchair the world became a much friendlier place, people were more understanding and they spoke to me more, it seemed as though they saw me more as a person than just a chap that came in every day, did his work and then went home.

A few months before this I was having a really bad day and I wanted to hide myself away from everyone. I went upstairs and went into a room and burst into tears. I didn't want anyone to see me but I heard the handle go down on the door, it was the Sergeant Major, he looked at me and could tell I had been crying. He left and went to his boss's office, Warrant Officer (WO2) Mike Collins. Mike came straight up to me. He took an hour out of his day to talk to me. That was a really important time for me. It was just before I had moved into my own place. I spoke to him at length and he understood everything I was saying. It was his job to make my workplace as comfortable as possible. After that everything got easier. My lack of mobility stopped being a problem for me and became one for my workplace to sort out. I remember reading the civil service benevolent fund literature. They assess people's work environment. I spoke to them and I told them I needed to start using a wheelchair and they sorted out one for me. They were instrumental in making me feel a lot happier about being at work. The main issue was beginning to use a wheelchair, and they funded it. In fact they were brilliant. At last, I began to feel like a disabled person and not feel like someone with a 'sort of problem'.

I really began to enjoy my work and enjoy speaking to everyone at this time. I was totally happy at 41 Sqn in Gale Bks and I can honestly say that it was down to the confidence I had gained in myself due to the use of the wheelchair. However after a few more years my responsibilities changed and a new computer system arrived which meant that all I was doing all day long was inputting data. I knew that with my newly found confidence I could look for another job within the MoD and apply for the job as a disabled person. It was no longer my worry about whether I could get into a new building or whether I could cope with the toilet or whether the stairs had rails by them. It was their problem, if they wanted to employ me then they had to make the changes required to accommodate me in my wheelchair.

We would get 'job bulletins' appearing in our in-trays every couple of weeks and I saw an interesting sounding job come up at 145 Bde. I didn't know who they were or what they did but the job looked right up my street. All figure work and calculation. That's what I was good at so I applied. The job was again in Aldershot, only about half a mile from Gale Bks. I was delighted to get an interview. This was with a Senior Civil Servant Doug Darvell. He told me that he had a young son who had autism and because of this he was only too aware that disabled people need to be given opportunities to be able to flourish. I then told him all about my ataxia, use of a wheelchair, improved confidence etc., etc. and he told me the job was mine but they would need to make some alterations like installing ramps by the entrance and putting in a disabled toilet. This was to be the one and only time in my career that my employer made any structural changes to the environment to accommodate me. We did not speak about the job at all which I found a bit strange. It was all about giving me an opportunity to prove myself.

Doug Darvell alone gave me that opportunity and I spent the best part of 7 years proving to him that I could do the job as well as anyone who didn't use a wheelchair. I was the only wheelchair user in the building and I would guess there were about 100 staff members including Civil Servants from grades AA (Admin Assistant) to SEO (Senior Executive Officer), Serving Soldiers from grades L/Cpl (Lance Corporal) to Bdr (Brigadier), retired officers and after having been there a few years, civilian Sodexho junior staff too. I felt immediately that I fitted in there. For the first time in my career I joined a unit feeling like a disabled person and not feeling like someone trying to hide something. While I was there this was accepted by all those mentioned and everyone understood that I needed a totally accessible environment and that as a full time wheelchair user I couldn't walk, carry drinks, climb stairs and needed to use the disabled toilet as opposed to the one everyone else used. This was no big deal for anyone and I just felt like one of the gang.

My job at 145 Bde was primarily to calculate the budget, in soldiers pay terms, of all units in the South East of the country that we were responsible for. I think the reason that Doug Darvell had not mentioned anything about the job was because he was aware that I would be working for a retired Officer called Major Moss. Major Moss, I later found out, had had seven previous clerks working for him and all seven had left within six months. I learnt the job from him within a few months and to be honest, once I had, I didn't really need his input in any way. However he loved interfering and telling me that I should be doing things another way. He became a huge annoyance and I began hating him, he spoke to me rudely and got me to do other work for him which he should have been doing himself. I used to try and avoid seeing him every day but like it or not, I was his clerk and my reason for being there was to help him in his duties.

I could feel him draining the confidence out of me day by day. I began losing sleep because I was worried about going in to work and having him watching over my every move. He had a very fast walk and I began feeling nervous and up-tight as soon as I heard his footsteps getting louder as he approached my office. The final straw came when he asked me to recalculate a whole set of figures to make it equal a certain amount. It was no good; I could not go on like this.

I think you should always give yourself six months in any job to see if you are going to enjoy it. When my six months were up I decided that if things stayed as they were I had to leave; just as my seven predecessors had. But I thought to myself 'Why should I?' I got on with everyone else, I could do the job I was employed to do, and I just could no longer work for this man.

I went to see the budget manager, the SEO that had interviewed me, Doug Darvell. He was on leave would you believe so I wrote a letter to him instead telling him exactly what Major Moss had asked me to do and that I would not go on working for him. I left it in his pigeon hole. When he returned from leave the next Monday he rang me and asked to see me in his office. He told me that he had received my letter and had decided to relocate me to the Budgets section. He would take the 'military pay' off Major Moss's duties and would bring in an EO (Executive Officer, a management grade, one grade above me) and I would in future be answerable to this new person.

That freed me from the grasp of Major Moss and I began to really enjoy work once more. I liked my job, enjoyed the responsibility I had and I got on well with both EO's that came in above me. I worked in the same office as first Chris and then Anne. They were both nice ladies although two totally different characters. They both allowed me to have the radio on all day which enabled me to keep up with what was happening in the world. I remember being in the office with Anne on 11th Sept 2001. It was Steve Wright (Radio 2) who first told me that a plane had crashed into one of the twin towers in New York. We didn't get much work done that afternoon!

Of course being in the same environment as 100 other people for eight hours a day, five days a week did mean that friendships between fellow colleagues did develop. Crystal worked in an office just outside the main building. In fact, it was a porta-cabin because 145 Bde had outgrown the building. I could obviously not get in there as there were steps with no

162

ramp. Having an attractive girl working in it wasn't really enough to warrant me throwing the disability discrimination card around. Our jobs never overlapped and so I had no reason to ever officially enter her office building. However I got to talk to her briefly as we went about our jobs on most days. She was very young, 17 when I first got to know her. I remember I took her to see the film 'Titanic' one evening and I used to give her a lift home when she rang our office to ask me. I can still remember many of our conversations now and when I made her laugh I would feel like I was on cloud nine. I spent many hours thinking about her instead of the job I was supposed to be doing. I was in my late 20's and used to think 'my dad is ten years older than my mum and they got together so 12 years difference is possible'. After a year or so of hiding my feelings for her I decided to let her know. So I wrote her a letter - and sent it to her home address. I didn't want her reading it with all her work-mates around her! I guess she got it as she never asked for a lift home again and although she didn't avoid me, we never really spoke properly again.

My last day in the MoD was in December 2002. A few years before that I had been finding my working days too physically demanding. I was starting to find that I was becoming too tired to be at work for the set eight hours (8.30-4.30) each day. I spoke with Anne my immediate boss about the possibility of reducing my hours. She sought permission from her bosses and it was agreed on the proviso that my workload remained the same. I was confident I could maintain the same workload per day with a one hour reduction so my request was granted. My employers (Sodexho) were doubtless quite pleased as they could reduce my monthly pay packet. So I continued working, arriving at work at 9.30am instead of 8.30am. In truth I rather enjoyed the extra hour in bed.

After about a year though - a year that included a personal house move - I began to realise that I felt far more able to cope with my life when I was at my new home. Here I could have things as I wanted them rather than in an office where my colleagues didn't have the same needs as me. I had an appointment with a counsellor at the Woking Community Hospital to help me decide if this thought was just a passing fad or something that would last. She suggested I saw a Dr McCluskie in the Rehabilitation Unit down the corridor. He was a neuro-rehabilitation clinician and his speciality - although I didn't know it at the time - was to advise patients on achieving outcomes so they can function as independently as possible, develop lifestyles as they choose and participate in the wider community. I explained to him that I felt more enabled while at home than I did at work and it was he who was the first person to suggest 'medical retirement.' I can help you achieve this, if that is what you chose to do' he said to me.

It seemed that medical retirement was not just something that happened to people that could no longer work but to people whose quality of life would improve for doing it. I had spent the whole of my life assuming the former but once the latter occurred to me I had no doubt that that was what I wanted. Dr McCluskie wrote to my employer in about the August of 2002 and by the end of the year I had my last day at work. I had to serve out 6 months on sick leave as medical retirement rules state that you can't pick up a wage one day and a retirement pension the next. So I picked up a full wage, well one hour a day short of a full wage for 6 months before my pension kicked in.

Work didn't change my lifestyle. After my A levels I never had time to twiddle my thumbs. My first proper job came along soon and other jobs just happened when I wanted them, in a sequence getting better each time. There was more job security and prospects for promotion back then I suppose, which helped.

Work was a social arena for me, especially after my ataxia had been diagnosed and I knew what I was talking about in relation to my disability. I got really friendly with John Ebbs who joined 41 Sqn at Gale Bks, we used to spend a lot time together and he came with me on holiday to Tenerife, to my ex-girlfriend Mel's funeral and he was with me when I did my parachute jump to raise money for Ataxia UK. He is 10 years younger than me and we are friends on Facebook now. Mike Collins, is another person who I was friends with. When I first saw him I wondered who he was and what he was doing here in my office. A corporal who worked closely with me and who I got to know quite well was with me in the office at the Detachment of the

Army School of Mechanical Transport at Deepcut stood to attention so I learnt he was someone important.

At Mons Bks I was put in an office with a female sergeant and a WO2. I didn't know them and it was a small office with the tables in a V shape in one corner. I sat in the corner of the V, so whenever I had to move I had to disturb people, which I hated. Bravely, I went into Captain England's office to ask if I could move the office around. He asked me why and I told him how unhappy I was having to disturb someone each time I wanted to move round the office. Much to my relief and satisfaction he said, "That's a very good question and very well presented" After this I became much more confident. I felt people had some understanding of my situation now. I wouldn't have had enough confidence to speak to people before but after that I could.

When I think about my working life I know that not every day was enjoyable, as many days were mundane and boring, but when I look back at the friends I made and the fact I had a place to go to and had a purpose and role in life, it was very good. Where I would have been today if I hadn't had these jobs, I do not know. Having work stopped me from being depressed and it served me well. When I was at 145 Bde, my employment was transferred to a civilian company Sodexo. They took over the management of lower grade MOD civil servants overnight. When I took Medical Retirement the benefits were very good. My terms and conditions when I retired were based on the highest salary over the last ten years multiplied by the time between starting with the company and the age 65. I took two pensions one from the MOD for 10 years work and one from the new company for 5 years work. This has enabled me to move forward in life and as my condition worsens provides me with a strong financial grounding.

Since leaving full time employment I have done mostly voluntary work apart from a few web designs. I've been working a bit on these, but not earning much or doing a lot. I used to do web design for 'Exclusive Beauty', I managed to get a contract with the chap who runs it. I was designing a website for another woman who organised parties for school kids, and I designed and I maintain a website for Chelsea Disabled Supporters Association.

I have my own personal website detailing my life, interests and travels and a website advertising my place over in Spain. I also write for Ataxia UK about issues relating to my life lived with ataxia. I have no desire to work but if I were forced to I would set up and run a Disabled Holidays Organisation. I have the experience with my house in Spain, (see Chapter 15) and could put this to good use.

Chapter 13.
Decision time.

Everyone makes a million and one decisions in their lives, a lot of them unconscious, arbitrary and in the moment. However, having a condition like ataxia means that as well as those everyday decisions being made, many life changing and life affirming ones have had to be faced by me throughout my life. Given that ataxia is a degenerative condition many of the big choices I have faced have been in direct response to a worsening of my ataxia, with its impact on my mobility and my balance. This chapter details a few of the major decisions I have made in order to maintain my independence and to keep safe.

For ease of reading I have decided to group the major decisions in my life into different categories: Early Decisions, Mobility Safety, Independence, Living Spaces and External Support. In these categories it is possible to see the progression of my condition and the decision process engendered by it.

Early Decisions

It was back in my teens when I had to make the first decision that would have a major impact on my life. I was an 'under 15s' footballer and at age 15, I made the decision to give up playing football for my Club team Curley Park Rangers. As with all the decisions that had an impact on my life. This one was made not because it was physically impossible to go on but ironically because I felt that through making it, my life would become less stressful and easier to manage. I knew what impact this decision would have on me and instinctively knew I had to 'soften the blow' or compensate myself in some way. As has been well documented in this book sport has always played a major role in my life, although now of course just as a spectator. To 'soften the blow' of not playing football anymore I threw myself into another sport - snooker. Every Sunday when I would have been playing football I was in my mate's garage playing snooker on a table that measured 5 foot by 2 1/2 feet in size. The last thing I was going to do was sit around the house thinking that at this time I would have been playing football for Curley Park. I also had to compensate for Saturday mornings when I would have been training, so I travelled up to London to watch the professional version of the game instead.

Mobility and Safety .

The first massive decision I made was when I was aged 22. I needed some sort of support when walking. I had become too worried about falling if I had to walk somewhere unaided. As I had been hiding my problems for some years, this was the first step finally in me being open about them. I reached the point in my life when the situation could not be brushed under the carpet. The process of getting some crutches, which I needed to improve my sense of safety, was undertaken by my parents after I told them for the first time of my problems with wobbliness and my need for help. This was a huge thing for me to do, but it broke the ice with them about what was going on for me. My dad approached Frimley Park Hospital, and got the crutches without any trouble; he may have fibbed a little to the hospital and said someone had broken their leg and as a result needed crutches. He borrowed them and only took them back when I got my wheelchair.

The crutches helped me immensely although trying to explain about why I was now using them could be quite difficult as I still had no real idea about what was wrong with me. I used to say "I have a problem with my balance which is so bad, I need crutches to help me." If people asked anything further I would just deflect the question, and people seemed to accept me as I was and it helped that they had seen me unbalanced before so it was a natural progression to have crutches. I still felt embarrassed though, as I didn't want to use them, it was just that I had to. This shame I felt was because, in fact, they slowed my walking down a lot, making me *more* conspicuous, not less so. Their function was to help with my balance and not just to keep one leg off the floor which meant I still needed to take things slowly to avoid falling. At first I only used them at work and even then only when I really had to. I used to use one of those office chairs with 5 castor wheels on the bottom to get around in the office. I used to lean my crutches neatly in the corner in the office, out of the way. Interestingly, I never used them at all at home. I used to stumble straight across the lawn at my parents' home from my car to the front door at this time and would use walls, chairs, radiators and anything else positioned correctly to get around in the house.

I began using crutches when I worked for 41 Sqn at Mons bks. I remember feeling extremely nervous when I first used them, not because of any difficulty with my balance as of course I was now less likely to fall over not more likely, but because of the bombardment of questions I thought I would be faced with. When I was working for 41 squadron at Gale Barracks a couple of years later , and as I touched upon in the 'My Travels chapter, I was approached by one of my colleagues, who was organising a works trip to France. She asked me if I would consider using a wheelchair for the day. She thought I would be better off and have more fun by using one. Her question was more likely to have been prompted by thoughts of improving everyone else's day in not having to wait for me all the time. My decision to say yes was massive and life changing. Up to that point I would have said no and probably not even have gone but since she had asked I thought what the hell? I had a wonderful day and felt so relaxed, as no one asked questions, and I no longer had to worry about keeping up with everyone. People were accommodating of me and I was more involved. Everyone at work realised that in not using the chair it would have been impossible for me to attend the works trip and everyone respected and accepted me for doing so. One of the benefits for instance was, I would not have had the courage to walk over to someone across a room on my crutches, but in the chair I just wheeled myself over to anyone I wanted to speak to. This event also helped me to push for a firm diagnosis, and I started to think immediately, that living my life in a wheelchair would be better, although I didn't want to just do it. I wanted finally to be told by a professional.

On the day of my ataxia diagnosis in January 1993, I realised that a wheelchair was imperative. I was told that it was best for me which exactly matched my own opinion. It is so important when making a decision of this magnitude to be ready for it and to know it is for the best. I was more than ready. The family went to Copenhagen in February 1993 for a 'Top 12' table tennis tournament and whilst there I used a hired wheelchair. I felt totally empowered and enjoyed the freedom it gave me. However, it had a squeaky wheel and I remember thinking wouldn't it be lovely if I had my own wheelchair which didn't squeak. It took time to get this permanent wheelchair though, but I got my own finally in May 1993 thanks to Sue Grice of Ataxia UK. This chair was called a Meteor and I used it immediately on a family holiday in Gothenburg, Sweden to watch the World Table Tennis Championship.

Another important decision for me was, having begun to feel unsafe in having a bath, was to install a shower. Literally it was getting in and out of the bath that was a problem which was seriously worrying me. As with all the decisions described in this chapter I think it is important for me to focus on only the immediate future and not to think back to how things were. This means my thoughts stay positive. 'This will make my life easier' is often what I say to myself. The change from bath to shower occurred after I had moved in to my first house, about two years later. I remember a feeling of freedom and self-reliance when I made this decision because it only affected me and it was my home so I could do what I wanted in it. No one else needed to know about it or even make a decision about it except me. I must say here that my local council (Surrey Heath) was on this occasion very speedy with arranging everything for me. They seemed to realise how important it was for me to maintain my personal hygiene, remain independent and be safe whilst doing it.

One of the biggest issues I face as a wheelchair user is 'falling' during a transfer from chair to bed or chair to toilet. When I fell out my chair or mucked up a transfer it used to cause me enormous frustration as I would try and try and try to get back into my chair. I would cry with frustration that I couldn't just get on with my day. I now have an emergency alarm which I can press and paramedics are round within 20 minutes to help me up. No tears, no frustration any more. Just half an hour lost from my day! Decision made: 'I can no longer get back into my chair' and solution organised.

Independence.

Another decision I reached was to move out of my parent's house. This decision was made shortly after my diagnosis of ataxia, but did not occur until 25th October 1993, 10 months later. Once I had started to use a wheelchair outside, it became obvious to my parents that I needed to use it in the house too. Access issues aside, I don't think they were aware how much they were doing for me, for, like any parent it was second nature to help their children. I longed to do lots of things for myself, but they would jump in for me with the best of intentions. So on a practical level mum was OK about me moving, but I am not sure about my dad. He was worried for me, I think. When I moved out, I did not even know how to make a cup of tea, so I can understand his anxiety. When I was diagnosed was the point at which I decided to take control of my situation. It was clearly impossible to use the chair at home as the front door had a step, the first of many no-no's which made the house unfit for purpose. The knowledge that I needed to use a wheelchair all the time and that the house was not right for me to do that, spurred me on in my decision to move out. I think over time I must have been watching mum and dad in order to gain the necessary skills, before moving out, thinking of all the situations I would face, and how I would do things.

Another major decision towards increased independence that I have made since being here in my new house is beginning to use a powerchair. This happened because I can remember when the sun was shining and the weather was warm I would be itching to go out and get around by myself and I couldn't in my manual wheelchair. This change has proven to be another positive decision for me.

Developing from this decision to use a power chair I recently decided to acquire a power / manual wheelchair which means I no longer need to be involved in so much transferring between chairs that I used to have to do when I had separate manual and power chairs.

Living Space.

Another choice I made was moving home from my first house in Chobham to Lightwater, the kitchen there was bad for me; the room was so narrow I could not turn around in it, which became a real irritation over time and it was so small I could not reach to all the places I was forced to store pots, pans, plates and cups. Also as irritating for me was not having broadband internet. I did not mention this to the council of course, as I don't think it would have been a good enough reason to re-house me in itself. You could say that I used the health and safety regulations to my advantage to secure the move. If the inadequate kitchen didn't do the trick then the 'one means of ingress/egress situation I found myself in in this house i.e. only having a front door, and not a back' did. This was a move for the better as I had had a lot of experience in my first home and could translate that into a new and better one. I guess it felt strange for the first couple of months as I was still working and had a different journey home. However my current house is more spacious, the whole environment is more accessible, it is much closer to my family and has a great, high speed internet connection!

External Support.

PA's started working for me towards the end of my time at Chobham, interestingly about the same time as I started to think about moving house. They were there initially to help me keep my house clean and tidy and help me cook healthy food and do a weekly shop, there being no online grocery shopping then. Of course having had PAs for 16 years I realise now that I could not live my life without them as I would be indoors all day every day, and that is no life. It was my decision to approach social services back in 1998 about the possibility of having them. It was a reasonably new concept back then. I am thus extremely grateful to the group of disabled people who fought for their right to choose who supplied their care back in the mid 1990's.

The future.....

A major future decision I hope I will not have to make, is the use of a catheter. The use of the toilet in the morning when I am busting for the loo was a massive issue for me, as my ataxia makes my movement more uncoordinated especially when working to a tight deadline. This urgency I felt was because I knew the practicalities involved in going to the toilet in the morning, [getting out of bed, transferring to my wheelchair, moving to the bathroom and transferring to the toilet] all of which in turn add to the problems I already felt in needing the loo. Thankfully, I recently had an appointment with a urologist at the Queens Square Neurology hospital and this is now sorted. This though is a bit like all the other decisions, I bury them in the back of mind for now and only work with them once they become imperative.

A long time into the future there may also be a need for an automatic patient turner device which could be both useful and necessary. Many decisions are needed as we all age but I think it best not to think about it right now. The only thing which is different for me is that these decisions can be accelerated because of my ataxia.

Making decisions and the skills needed to do so.

My advice to someone else about decision making, is, I would say, to treat everything on a day to day basis. It is impossible to make a decision about something that may not even happen. You would not get a handrail on your stairs when you are 25 in preparation for being aged 80. Just decide as and when things become necessary. The professionals might make you believe in one thing but don't believe in it - only believe in what your own mind and body is telling you. Don't be dictated to by someone who thinks they know what is best for you. You can push yourself and as the world is now a much friendlier place for disabled people this can make more things possible. There is legislation to protect the rights of disabled people and attitudes have also changed.

You need to be able to think ahead but not ahead too far, - a month or a year ahead but not five or ten years ahead. You need to think how to make your life easier. Sharing information about your problems and seeking professional help is vital. You can record what the problem is over time and in detail. For instance, I talked to a PA about my toilet issues in the morning. She has children, and she has experienced similar problems as a mother with them and was able to discuss solutions with me. I then had a pad on my wheelchair seat to protect the chair until I could sort something else out with a specialist.

If I hadn't been the person I am I would probably have been in a coffin long ago. I personally do not know how people can be passive when they are told they have a disability. For me it would be as though I would have looked forward to 30 years of being in a 'giving up' mode, which for me would be a real downer. I would have been totally dependent on PAs or worse still my parents and I would have had no energy or self-belief. I would hate to think of where I would have been if I still had the thoughts I had when I was 18. The diagnosis was the difference, the catalyst for getting on with my life. All the people I met after that and all the information I was given spurred me on from that moment. Don't get me wrong - I could have responded differently and I totally understand how easy it can be to give up. I just flipped it on its head and decided to treat the knowledge of my disability as a positive thing.

Maintaining my independence has always and will continue to be a challenge for me. It has become a constant way of challenging myself in finding the easiest ways to do things and is a focal point in managing my life. I have learnt over the years of employing PA's however that being independent does not necessarily mean doing everything yourself. Independence is achieved when someone you choose does something for you in the way you want. The big thing with ataxia is wondering how long it is possible to go on doing things the way you always have. I know I will maintain 100% independence whilst continuing to make decisions and changes in my life even if some of these changes are unwanted.

Chapter 14.

Ataxia UK.

'Ataxia is a name given to a group of neurological disorders that affect balance, coordination and speech.'

(Ataxia UK website, http://www.ataxia.org.uk)

Ataxia UK started out as FAG (the Friedreich's Ataxia Group) in the mid-1960's, and involved a small number of parents and carers of those with ataxia who met for mutual support. This formal title is the name I first knew it by, following my diagnosis of Friedreich's Ataxia, as it only changed to the more upbeat name in 1997. For the sake of brevity and to avoid confusion, I will refer to the charity as Ataxia UK from now on. Over the years much has changed, not just the name. For instance in 1988 the scope of the charity's work broadened to include all forms of cerebellar ataxia. This was also the year that saw Sue Chamberlain and her team finally locate the gene for Friedreich's ataxia on Chromosome 9, something which underpins all research into the condition.

The charity is funded by voluntary contributions and has been able to give millions of pounds towards research. One of the two current missions of Ataxia UK is to maintain the services they manage and continue to develop; these are the helpline, free information and published resources, regular national and regional events and the Medical Advisory Panel.

Of course the other important mission of Ataxia UK is the support they provide to research into finding a cure. Much research is being undertaken into Friedreich's ataxia worldwide and is focussed on a range of issues associated with the condition including: the deficiency of the protein Frataxin; the accumulation of free iron which results from the deficiency of the protein; the increased susceptibility to oxidative stress engendered by the two previous issues; the treatment of the condition with Vitamin E and

Coenzyme Q10; the use of synthetic antioxidants and even stem cell and other genetic interventions. Some of these research projects are showing some improvements in the neurological conditions of individuals but often not a measurable difference between those taking the treatments and those being given placebos. The Ataxia UK website has a mass of material about the condition and the various research projects being developed around the world.

My own involvement with Ataxia UK began within a week of receiving my diagnosis in 1993, with both me and my mum separately contacting the charity. There were 4 staff members then: Sue, who kindly took the calls from me and my mum, Chrissy, Vicky and David. They were based in Elstead, Godalming, Surrey and as I worked in Aldershot, Hampshire at the time, which is about half an hour's drive away, I used to drive over there about once a month during my lunch break. My employers understood the importance of these regular visits as they recognised the change in my character and mood and never questioned the two hours I was away when I just had an hour for lunch.

The first thing that Ataxia UK did was to make me realise that I was not alone and soon they put me in touch with others who had ataxia. This enabled me to make friends with people who I could talk to about the things I had been and was now going through. They were an amazing support for me at what was a frightening and confusing time. They encouraged me to discuss my feelings around my diagnosis and discuss the symptoms of my ataxia from the early stages. I had only ever had my diary to confide in before and to be able to talk to other people about what I had been going through was extremely important and life enhancing. It was very comforting to be understood by them and to be told that my feelings were normal. In April of this same year they organised a 'Talk In' weekend, to which families of those affected by the condition, including my mum and dad, were invited and encouraged to 'open up' to other families in a similar position.

In the first few years following my diagnosis, Ataxia UK played a significant part in my life. I was encouraged to become 'The face of a newly diagnosed young man' for them and I featured prominently in their magazine and attended a few events where I represented them. I remember the opening of a restaurant in which all profits would go to Ataxia UK where I got to sit next to Kim Wilde [Pic 15], the pop star and I even attended a 'suit and tie' charity event to raise funds for them [Pic 21].

As well as being involved in publicity for the charity I also became a 'point of contact' for people with Ataxia or who supported someone with the condition. I particularly enjoyed speaking to newly diagnosed youngsters, who were like I had been before my diagnosis: all full of confusion and denial, and I tried to encourage them to talk.

On a more practical note I have raised money for them - by having the Friedreich's ataxia Group tattooed on my arm, with a Chelsea FC club badge on the other [Pic 8] by jumping out of a plane at 15,000 feet [Pics 11&14] and by sitting outside supermarkets holding collection boxes. I was also their webmaster for three or four years updating their website with information and for many years I wrote articles in their magazine talking about going online to help with life's' practicalities, useful websites and how the internet can help disabled people and particularly those affected by ataxia.

Something which meant a lot to me and which has fuelled my desire to write this book, is the time I spent as a writer for the Ataxia UK magazine. I thoroughly enjoyed this work. I wrote an article for every edition of the quarterly magazine between 2001-2006. The editor trusted me to write about what I thought benefitted others with ataxia and she usually published pretty much exactly what I had written. Unfortunately with a change of editor, I lost this freedom as the new editor chopped and changed what I had written and even added many of her own thoughts. Most writers will tell you that this is something that is hard to stomach, so I stopped writing for them. There is now a new editor who gives me freedom once more and I now write an article each issue entitled 'Adapting to life with ataxia' where again I discuss life's ever-changing practicalities when you have ataxia.

Whilst I had been writing for the magazine, Ataxia UK conducted surveys of what readers liked in the magazine and my webmaster articles were the 3rd most favoured articles. This encouraged me immensely. I even got an email from the now late Peter Cordwell, a writer on the subject of ataxia, saying how much he enjoyed reading my articles. Peter was once the UK representative of Euro-Ataxia, a Europe-wide campaigning and support organisation, and once he invited me to join him at a meeting in Amsterdam. I went along and soon afterwards Peter asked me to take on his duties. After some thought I declined this invitation and in a subsequent email he said I chose correctly as I had already chosen the right 'niche' for myself by writing for the magazine. I valued his opinion greatly.

Generally my relationship with Ataxia UK has been consistently good. In fact when the charity was small I would say it was better than good - it felt like a kind of family. Since the charity has grown and changed its base to London, it has become more commercial and is run as a professional organisation. In my view it is now less concerned with supporting individuals that have ataxia and more concerned with research and finding a cure, although of course that is very important. Thankfully though for people living with ataxia there are strong networks nationally to get some peer support. I am clear though that my personal opinion about the focus of Ataxia UK could be based on the fact that I have become used to living with ataxia and so need less support. The relationships I have developed with Ataxia UK have been based really on connections built up with people that work there, initially Sue Grice and now Sheila Benneyworth, the helpline and Friends Services Manager. To me, these people *are* the charity because they deal with the people that have ataxia. The charity now has a chairman, a chief executive, a finance manager, a branch development manager and many other posts. This is par for the course with any large charity but to me, I preferred it being little old FAG, oops I said I wouldn't mention FAG again, but I think I need to here to make a point!

In my view, as someone who has used the services of and worked for Ataxia

UK, it is a thriving, successful and professionally run charitable organisation. It has grown hugely since I first became involved with them and they provide an invaluable service to anyone who has a connection with ataxia and especially to those affected by the condition and their families. Personally though, I now have less to do with them, although I do still contact them occasionally, and I know they are always there, but I guess I need them less as the years go on. I would though like to acknowledge and thank them for having a huge impact on my life especially during the first few years immediately following my diagnosis. They continue to be very important to me and I am clear that without them I would not be who I am today.

Chapter 15.

My Spanish Home.

In July 2008 a good friend of mine and fellow ataxian Greer Watson went to Garrucha in Spain with the specific aim of finding a suitable property to purchase. This was intended to become both a holiday home for her and her family and also a 'home from home' for me, my family and my friends to visit regularly. Having been to Spain on holidays before it seemed the obvious choice for a holiday home. It is only two and a half hours away by plane which I can cope with and of course the climate is massively different from here with warm sunshine beating down all year. We got in touch with an estate agent there and told her where we were looking for a place and the things that we needed to have in the property because of our disabilities.

We looked at a few available properties in Garrucha but none seemed suitable so we took a 90 minute drive northwards to look at some properties near Mazarron. We looked at a few villas in an urbanisation called The Country Club which is located in the hills close to the town and we saw what we regarded as a suitable property. The Country Club has about 800 homes on it and is built around an attractive central avenue. It consists of various types of properties, from small bungalows to large detached villas. A lot of people have holiday homes and some people live there. Most of the people are expats from all over Europe. We liked the Town of Mazarron, we liked the idea of being on an urbanisation and we liked the bungalow. So the estate agent set the wheels in motion to buy it and we eventually exchanged contracts in January 2009.

A couple from Norway live next door one way and an English lady the other. There is a strong community of owners who meet regularly and are very open and transparent in the way they operate. I didn't realise what an advantage it would be to have the Country Club's support - they take care of security, and maintenance and are predominantly English speaking which is a real help. They give all the owners like myself a strong say in what goes on there. It is a friendly environment, and whenever you go out you are sure to meet others from the estate who are only too willing to stop and chat.

Greer, the person with whom I first bought the villa in Spain, has been a friend of mine for about 15 years and she has ataxia too. We met through her sister Fay, who also has ataxia, whom I had met through Ataxia UK. Greer is 5 years older than Fay and I always got on better with her.

If it wasn't for Greer I could not have afforded to buy the villa. She had to apply for a mortgage which she was successful in getting and this made it all possible. The whole idea for me came about because in the middle of 2008 my grandad died. Mum and Dad inherited half of his estate, which was a large bungalow. They asked me if they could buy the bungalow for me as somewhere I could live to be independent, but I didn't feel I could sort all the accessibility issues out there. Also with my own home, which is rented, I could get repairs done by the council. Instead of them letting me have the bungalow though, I asked if they would give me the money to buy a house in Spain, which they kindly did.

When we first acquired the property, there was a patio outside the front door which was a foot high. This meant we could not get to the front door. The first job then was to get at the side of the bungalow, a smooth pathway from the road all the way up the side of the bungalow and after that, to get a ramp on the side of the patio to enable ourselves to access the front door. When we got the ramp up to the patio, I was concerned about legislation to change the appearance of the property, but apparently as long as the footprint of the building doesn't change it is OK. Some of the other access issues inside have been dealt with over time and this work is obviously ongoing as is the work in my UK home, according to my changing needs. There was a bit of wall sticking out between the kitchen and the lounge so that has gone now, and also a wall from the bathroom to the bedroom has gone to increase the size of the passageway. The bathroom also used to have a cubicle shower, and that was then taken away and I got a drop down shower chair and a smaller sink fitted. Greer did most of the girly things, like decoration and chattels, the cutlery and crockery etc. She also got the dining room table, TV, TV stand and sofa-bed and I got the internet which is now accessible with Wi-Fi. Recent changes include the bedroom door being made a bit wider and the bathroom floor being re-laid. There may well come a time, when the kitchen needs to be made accessible. It would be a big job though as it would involve building at the back of the house where there is very little space. In 2011 we bought the other half of the villa from Greer so my family now owns the whole house and I am free to use the place whenever I like.

Our times at the house have not always been about access and modifications. There have been many good and funny times. While on holiday there with a friend of mine, Katie (who also has ataxia) and our two PA's, we were both sitting having a drink after dinner. I sipped my drink and placed the glass back on the table. I then swallowed and coughed, hitting my knees on the underside of the table. Katie's startled reaction whilst she was holding her drink made her throw her drink all over the floor. We both laughed thinking 'It could only happen if it were two ataxians.

I love the villa because for me it is like having a home from home, and I know that when I get there everything will be the way I want it to be. I have the same bed as my one in the UK and two floor to ceiling poles. Dad shipped them all to Mazarron for us as he deals with shipping things to different places in his work. Paul, my friend and PA, fitted one pole by my bed and the other is a spare to be used when and if the need arises. Paul also put the adjustable bed together for me. The fact that the villa has two bedrooms, one of which has the capacity for an extra bed making it a twin room, affords me the opportunity, as it does other people with disabilities who stay there, to bring along PAs to help them maybe more than they normally would i.e. with putting our clothes on for us. It is a place for me to have a holiday after all and I relish this fact. It is lovely for me not to have to put my own clothes on like I do every day in the UK. It is a rest for me; a proper holiday. However, it makes me a bit anxious when I get home though and I have to do my own stuff, but I enjoy the break. In 2010 I visited 6 times but now less often as I have trouble getting PAs to go with me.

I rent out the villa to other people with disabilities and probably have two or three visitors a year. I had an English couple next door, Jan and Clive, although Clive died in 2011, which meant Jan wanted her sister to stay with her for 6 months, which she did, in the villa. The villa though is not like a business, which makes it more of a holiday-time investment. Having said that I do advertise the property on two accessible holiday websites and me having ataxia means I have a lifetime of coping strategies under my belt, so that anyone with ataxia who wants somewhere to stay will find place ideal. I currently only recommend the villa to disabled people, but the place can be rented to others as well. My parents recently visited the villa and found a golf club and suggested I advertise to golfers.

When other people use the villa we provide a few basic pieces of equipment such as a shower chair (although people may wish to use the shower in the private back courtyard which is fitted out for this purpose), a transfer board, a standing frame, a patient turner and a range of fixed accessible equipment throughout the bungalow. Also thanks to a local mobility company many other devices are available to hire at competitive prices. There is also a fantastic medical service in Spain but if you are from the UK, you must take your EHIC card to access the services.

Back in July 2008 when we decided to buy the place, one of the main reasons I liked it was Puerto de Mazarron, the resort, which is a 10-15 minute drive from my place and it is very accessible, even the promenades and beaches. In High Season they put out wooden pathways making the sea accessible for wheelchair users. The restaurants are all accessible too. This is a boon place for me. There are good supermarkets, take away restaurants and loads of outdoor cafes overlooking the water. There are basically great amenities with even DIY shops.

When I am there I like to do lots of things. There is a zoo in Murcia and the beaches of course. A ten minute drive in the opposite direction to Puerto takes you to our neighbouring urbanisation called Campersol where we watch football in the cafes and go out for dinners. I have even been swimming at the Country Club pool which is more than just usable but perfectly fit for purpose. The whole end of the communal pool is a ramp. I bought a shower wheelchair from eBay and use it along with a rubber ring and I get pushed down the ramp until the water becomes deep enough for me to just float off. It is a perfect activity for a disabled person.

The estate agent that we bought the villa from, Caroline looked after the place for us and her partner Martin, did a lot of work for us on the house. Caroline and her partner have moved away now so I asked for some help to find someone else, and she gave me a phone number of someone called Clare who did the handovers until recently. She had a contact, a builder who will most likely do new work for me as well which is great. I now have another person Alison who takes care of the place and does the handovers. All these things take time in Spain though so I am having to learn to be patient. As with my life in the UK, I manage all the bookings, maintenance and advertising myself.

I have no plans to make drastic changes to the property although I was hoping that Jan might move out and the family could buy her house, especially as they have a swimming pool. That seems unlikely to happen now though. The villa has in fact fallen in value, but as Paramount are planning a theme park nearby and a new international airport is due to open closely too, the values should go up.

If I could go to the villa without worrying anyone else, it would be fantastic. I am a little restricted due to a lack of PA's who are willing and able to travel with me. I would go more often if I could get the PAs but not necessarily for longer. It's only a 2.5 hour flight so it's easy to go at any time. It may be possible to recruit someone specifically to go to Spain with me, but the most important factor in that is my being able to get on with them. Having said that, I love to just pack up and get away. I know that when I get there everything will be familiar and I will have nothing to worry about.

Chapter 16.

My Future.

'I have thought a lot about my problem today - I prefer to call it a problem rather than a disease because I feel it is something I must overcome. The disease cannot be cured; a problem can.'

In a way, I think the best way to start this chapter about My Future is to hark back to my past. Rather like other children, mourning is not something that I was aware of in relation to the changes that I was experiencing in my body after the age of thirteen. That doesn't mean I wasn't lamenting the incremental losses in my physical abilities at some level though. In order to recognise my emotions as they related to my condition I did once have genetic counselling after my diagnosis but this only served to confirm that my thought processes about my condition were all normal. So in effect, I got little from the session and have never had more since. It is only with the passing of time and my deteriorating physical condition that I can recognise the losses I have experienced and make some sense of them as I reside in my present and move into my future.

The positive difference for me now is that I have a long standing and correct diagnosis so I can better mentally plan for my current circumstances and for any future changes. For many years before my diagnosis of ataxia I was only able to address changes in a knee-jerk and arbitrary way as I had no idea what was happening to me; the diagnosis enabled me to think more strategically. Having said that, my overarching philosophy is: don't focus too far ahead. I think there is no point in worrying about what condition you are going to be in. I always try to live in the present only. However, conversely, you do still need to plan a certain degree ahead to keep your life running as best it can. For instance, I need to realise that it is difficult to transfer between my wheelchairs, so I need a combination chair now, which I have recently purchased.

I believe the best way is to try to make my life as easy as possible for myself right now, without giving in to the condition before I need to. I think this ethos must have been in me as a child because I have really been dealing with the effects of the condition from the ages 15 to 22 and no one taught me how to do it. I think as a young child one cannot look too far ahead and I have carried this on into my adult life. I had to make my first life changing decision to use crutches to help me walk and that was me thinking ahead to some degree, but not thinking long term as that was ultimately to be the change to using a wheelchair and I hadn't even thought of that back then. When I was 17-18, my peers all started looking ahead, but with my Ataxia (or CMT as it was then), I didn't want to know. I instead simply chose a day to day existence. I was conscious that something was wrong but I didn't know how to think about it. I look back now and I can honestly say I didn't worry too much. I had an alternative life that was bestowed on me - not ideal, but it was at least in *my* control.

The main thing I have wanted to get across in this book is the notion that, and this applies to everyone disabled or not, *'Don't look too far ahead, just think only day to day.'* In my life in general I find I can only really think about how I am at the moment. I remember years and years ago, post my ataxia diagnosis, I went with Lee, my sister Louise's ex-husband, to watch Chelsea play at Oldham, an F A Cup match which Chelsea won 2-0. On the way back Lee took me to see his dying brother Graham and he was wearing his Manchester United shirt and I said jokingly "You can take that off for a start". I figured he might appreciate a joke rather than a sad face in that moment. When we got home to my mum and dad's house, Lee had to get my chair out of the boot. He said "Do you not get frustrated? Everyone else would have sat down to dinner in the time it took you to get out of the car." My comment was: "It is not a race, I just need time to get things done and I have to accept that." I had known him from the age 15, and he had seen my deteriorating condition and yet he didn't have a clue about it really. Once I had a wheelchair, he just noticed the time it was taking me to do things, that is all. Maybe he was noting the time it was taking 'him' to help me, as perhaps he was eager to eat his dinner! Even my nieces have both commented on how long it takes me to get out of the car and into the house. I wonder why?

I have always been a practically minded person and I have always regarded every problem as a challenge and every true challenger has a way of solving problems. I get the impression that no one knows my own body as well as I do, and that includes all the professionals who are involved with ataxia even the top experts in the world. They can still not tell me a better way of doing things, and everyone copes best with their own problems I believe. For example, I know better than an Occupational Therapist (OT) what I want and need. When I saw an OT the last time, I asked if my toilet could be lowered by an inch and she told me rather than lower it I ought to raise my knees up further when I slide from chair to toilet and that she would find me a device to assist me with that. What a joke - she had absolutely no idea how I transferred to the toilet and I just wasn't going to demonstrate or explain. She measured the toilet to the floor and said "That is fine, no problem." What she didn't understand and never asked me about is, when I get out of my chair onto the toilet I don't slide, like other people might do, I use my arms to pull myself up on the floor-to-ceiling pole, and raise myself to standing position, twist and fall onto the toilet, thereby not transferring at all, but instead lifting, twisting and plonking myself down. Alternatively, a paraplegic person would transfer in the normal way but not a person with ataxia. I never heard another thing from her, she had done her job and saved money for the council. I paid £300 to the toilet installers to lower it by installing a 2 inch plinth instead of the 3 inch one that was there already

I, like many other people with ataxia, am not the textbook disabled person. The OT Department wants to set things up for textbook cases only, not people with ataxia. People with ataxia may have limited use of their legs but are able to lift themselves up using the strength in their arms and then use their legs to hold themselves up. Their problems are coordination and balance, so how I was supposed to use some leg lifting device when I am already struggling to balance myself. As I said. I think finance is usually the reason for OTs to provide a limited range of solutions. They go for what is the easiest or the simplest or cheapest and not what is best for the person. To give them their due, the more senior ataxia experts have a broader view and agree that people with ataxia must formulate their own philosophy. I though have never thought about that from any other point of view.

The important thing I have learnt in my life is to get to know the right people to approach to make the system work in your favour. I was on the phone daily when my new Lightwater home was being adapted for me. I got to know the social worker very well. I wanted to know how things were progressing and how it was being funded. I believe it is useful to be involved with everything. I think generally people have realised my philosophy on life pretty early, so they soon learn there is no point in arguing with me, in fact it is a lost cause. I know my own mind after all. People can ask me what I want, indeed I appreciate that, but don't try to tell me. I insist on being on the case and I made it apparent that I would expect everything to be right, from workmen and OTs. I described to my builders the layout of my new kitchen and that I wanted a breakfast bar and needed a wall knocking down to accommodate my plans. I visited the empty home as the builders were working on it one day, out of the blue, and noticed that the breakfast bar table was 2 inches too high. I said "There is no way I can eat my dinner on that table every day for the rest of my life." I knew straight away that the table was not the height I had asked for. The builders made an excuse but I insisted that they drop it, which they did! It is why I went round to check on them. Another thing that happened was they had laid the kitchen floor, in solid flooring, but only in the kitchen. I said "I want that laid all the way up to and under the breakfast bar table", in fact twice the length of the kitchen. They had to re-order the material because they had assumed I would only want it in what was once just the kitchen and had not checked with me before ordering the materials. People had to see I would not take things less than perfect and once they understood that, things ran smoothly.

One way a council OT did benefit me once, was when one of them took me to a designer for accessible kitchens in High Wycombe. The designer was a wheelchair user himself and he virtually told me exactly how I should have the kitchen set up in order to make things as easy as possible for me. He planned my kitchen down to the last detail. He did not have ataxia and was surprised at some of the design I wanted, but generally he was an expert and I was a beginner so I noted everything he said. The OT came straight back to my home in Chobham and immediately rang the builders and gave them all the designer's plans. A few weeks later the designer from High Wycombe found out about this and went livid, as he had intended to get the job himself, and as a result he gave the OT a right talking to and made a complaint which resulted in the OT leaving her job. I must say though that on this occasion the OT's role was really beneficial to me even if to her it proved to be one of her last roles. Other than that, OTs have been pretty useless. I have to use them for financial reasons to get council money to do things but if I had my way I would never use an OT again.

Thinking about my life now, and as I age, things will always become more and more physically difficult for me, but it does me no good to think too far ahead and it is best to only concentrate on the 'here and now' (the present). My practical needs seem to be taking up more and more of my time. There never seems to be enough hours in the day. I could do with 30 hours to everyone else's 24! Of course on top of everything else I have been writing this book! Getting dressed in the mornings and stripping off for bed at night takes time, washing, cleaning my teeth, shaving all take time and they take longer and longer as the years go on. I have recently given up driving at night, not because of my driving abilities, but because of the problems the darkness brings in getting into and out of the car and to the steering wheel. Cooking meals for myself is now beyond difficult, due to my hands being very sensitive when I touch anything hot. My 'startled reaction' caused me to drop so many things that it was just no longer worth making the effort. Once when I was walking between cars stopped in a queue on a road near the Oval cricket ground, when walking was difficult but possible, and I could use stopped cars to hold onto, to keep my balance, someone beeped their horn and I was so startled I lost control of my limbs and fell over in the middle of the road.

This 'startled reaction' happens a lot as I have an involuntary physical reaction to surprise moves or sounds. Balancing while sitting forward and using a knife in one hand and a fork in the other is becoming problematical too. It is far easier for food to be cut up so that I can eat it with just a fork and leaving my left hand free to balance myself. I'd never considered years ago that balance would be an issue when I was eating, but it now is. When a dinner table does not have access under it this can be a big problem too as my leg-rests need to be removed giving me nothing to put my feet on for balance. So all in all, keeping me safe and well balanced is quite a complex

189

As well as practical changes that I am experiencing I also am having to learn and accept the emotional impact of how to consent to greater levels of support. I have always been and continue to be a very proud person. I can manage everything myself if I have enough time. My life now is such that I do need help because as I said before I don't get 30 hours in a day, I get only 24 like everyone else. So in order to achieve all that I want to I must accept more help. Also people cannot wait for me to do things, within the limited hours I employ them, so they must help me. I am aware if I insist on doing things for myself then I pay the price for my independence. For example, packets of food make life difficult for me but when I am alone I soldier on with them. I think I have no choice so I had better get on with it.

The future, I do not dwell on too much. I would like to be able to go to South America and see the next Olympics in Brazil. It is a 12 hour flight and I will need a toilet, which makes it very difficult. I could do it in stages, I suppose as I haven't flown for more than 4 hours for over ten years. I could go by sea maybe, like a cruise. This could be a good thing even though it takes a week to get there. However, taking longer wouldn't worry me as my pace of life is slow and in 'the now'.

There are without doubt things in my life that I could mourn: playing competitive sports; walking; having a bath; working; having the ability to climb back into my wheelchair when I have fallen from it and hearing properly as I have Auditory Neuropathy Spectrum Disorder due to my ataxia causing deterioration of the cochlea in my ear. This means I can't distinguish between background noise and the spoken word. However, I have chosen immediately, when the need has arisen, to focus instead on coping without them. I have also always found it very difficult to compare my life to that of others. I think most people would find it understandable how looking at my life and those of my school-friends and similarly-aged family members who have not had ataxia to contend with, can make me feel very down. It becomes more and more difficult over time as the only changes to my life are all geared around my increasing care needs and abilities, whereas my friends are entering new relationships, having children, and changing jobs.

I think it is natural for me with my ataxia to feel down at times. However, when I am feeling low I think of the things in my life that make me happy. These are materialistic things such as my home and its contents and also the independence that I still have. I simply do not think too far ahead but focus on what my life and ataxia throws at me day to day. This attitude gives me the strength and resilience to carry on with my life in a positive way meeting the challenges head on and with alacrity.

My future is the end of today or the week at most.

Matthew Law. 2014

Published by Duality Books

The Monograph Series. (so far...)

1.'Lines' by Edson Filho.

2. EXHIB / Hide by Luc Langrand

3. Mágnes / Magnet by Ágnes Mezősi

'Life Goes On. A photographic Book Exploring Ordinary Lives as lived during WWI.

Sachet Mixte - a collection of works by male artists. ~ Editions One, Two and Three.

'Coming To'- a novel: the Self-realisation of a Middle Aged Man.

'#geekG@d' - a novel.

'France in Ruins' - a study of the the culture of Ruination in France.

'Taking the Medicine' - a political play.

'Sunshine and Rain' - a children's story of healing.

'The Sea Urchin and the Shark' - a children's story of love.

In Development:

'Dwarves at Court' - a children's story..

'Endérin' - a psychic novel.

'Innusiq' - a children's story of a little bear who knew he was different.....

'Bandar' - an illustrated story, set in India, where a monkey causes havoc...

www.dualitybooks.com—for all your publishing needs.

6534243R00107

Printed in Great Britain
by Amazon.co.uk, Ltd.,
Marston Gate.